7 STEPS
TO SUCCESS

In Deen & Dunya

for Muslim Entrepreneurs,

Professionals, & Seekers

Maruf Yusuf

Please, send an email to salam@deenpreneurs.net to
give your feedback to improve the book,
order it wholesale, or
translate it to another language.

This book comes with bonuses.
If you ordered on www.deenpreneurs.net/book,
you already received it via email.

Otherwise, you can get your digital copy
and claim your bonuses here
www.deenpreneurs.net/book

Book Ver.: 2023.09.17

DEDICATION

Here's to the Deenpreneurs
who place Purpose over Profit
to serve The One by serving People

REVIEWS FROM MUSLIM COMMUNITY LEADERS

Imam Dr. Mustafa Khattab
Translator "The Clear Quran"

Ustaz Maruf has written a motivational, faith-based guide backed by extensive experience, Islamic insights & profound stories. A must-read for anyone who aspires to achieve their full potential and gain material success in this world and heavenly blessings in the Hereafter.

Shelina Janmohamed
VP of Islamic Marketing at Ogilvy, Author "Generation M"

It is an inspiring book that puts purpose at the heart of business success, and how to harness it for real impact. You'll get goosebumps when you read it.

Mohammed Qahtani
World Champion of Public Speaking, Public speaker

7 Steps to Success in Deen and Dunya is a simple & easy read with a vivid story to learn from. Maruf did an amazing job taking the reader through this journey.

Khalid Parekh
AMSYS GROUP, Founder, Chairman & CEO

A transformative book that teaches Muslim entrepreneurs to view their lives & work through a lens of possibility and abundance, rather than limitation and scarcity. Through inspiring stories and practical steps, Maruf encourages readers to tap into their creativity & unlock their full potential.

Na'ima B. Robert
Award-winning Author & Book Coach, Sisters Magazine Editor

I am so excited to finally see a book offering guidance to Muslims on how to profit from the online space - and in line with their purpose and passions, too! The fact that it is written by one of the halal industry's top experts, Maruf Yusuf, makes it even better. A must-read for anyone who has dreamt of starting a business in the digital age.

CONTENTS

ACKNOWLEDGMENTS

Alhamdulillah. Writing a book is harder than I thought and more rewarding than I could have ever imagined. I have to start by thanking these two awesome ladies in my life: my mom and my wife. Thank you, mom, for everything and for keeping me in your dua's. Thank you to my awesome wife, Kate, for giving me advice on the cover and keeping the minions out of my hair so I could edit; you are as important to this book getting done as I was. Thank you so much, dear!

I'm also thankful to my three minions who understood that their dad couldn't be with them as much as possible while writing this book. Yet they did this sacrifice understanding that it is for the greater good, inshaAllah.

I am grateful to Sakeena Rashid who patiently watched our Zoom sessions, listened to my audio recordings, transcribed them, and helped me to put the first early draft of this book.

I am also grateful to my editor sr. Kelly El-Yacoubi, who dotted the i's and crossed the t's to make sure that ideas are clear and communicated effectively to every reader.

I thank Imam Dr. Mustafa Khattab, Imam Suhaib Webb & Shaykh Faraz Rabbani for checking and making sure that I am not stepping out of the line of Islam.

I also thank sr. Na'ima Roberts, Coach Chihab Kaab, br. Laziz Rasulov & br. Omar Mboudu, sr. Hajera Memon for reading the early drafts and giving their feedback to make it better.

I am grateful to Shahbaz Mirza, Shelina Janmohammed, Junaid Wahedna, Khalid Parekh, Farooq Sayfutdin, Mohammed Qahtani, Isam Bachiri, Joe Bradford, and Ibrahim Khan, Chris Blauvelt for sharing their advice, stories, and feedback.

Finally, to all those who have been a part of my getting there: Mr. Selim Vural, Ulugbek Ustoz (rahimahullah), Sh. Muhammad Alshareef (rahimahullah), and all my other teachers, mentors, advisors, friends, fellow Muslim entrepreneurs and community leaders, teammates, and all who helped me on my journey.

In the Name of Allah

The Most Kind

The Most Caring

Introduction

Assalamu alaykum!

My name is Maruf. Nice to meet you. Thank you for being here.

Right now, you could be watching some cute kittens on YouTube. You could be binging your favorite show on Netflix. Or you could be doing what you usually do to kill time. Actually, time is slowly killing us all.

Yet you are here. I honor you and I honor your time. I will do my best to make sure it is worthwhile, inshaAllah.

You've probably done the things mentioned above over and over. We all have. But they never leave us fulfilled. At the end of the day, something deep inside calls. It calls for something larger than yourself.

There is a candle in your heart, ready to be kindled. There is a void in your soul, ready to be filled. You feel it, don't you?
—Rumi

Have you ever wondered why we love stories, especially underdog stories?

For example, how Dawud (AS) overcame Jalut.

Somehow, most people treat reality - our everyday life - as something mundane and boring. So most people escape by "killing time" in the form of alternate realities.

For some, it is drugs and alcohol. For some, it is entertainment. For some, it is something else. Anything but the reality itself.

In this book, we will look into this "broken" reality and see if we missed something. Is there a way to live where you thrive instead of survive? Is there a way to live so you don't have to escape your everyday life? Is there a way to live so you love what you do and do what you love and make a good living doing that?

Sounds too good to be true? Hold on to this thought. We will come back to this. I feel you. I have been there. I promise it will be worthwhile.

Meanwhile, we have some burning questions to answer.

Questions

Before we get started on our journey, I want to address some of the questions you may be asking, so you know why you should stick with me along this journey.

You may ask yourself: "What is this book all about? Why did this guy write this book? Why should I care or bother reading it? Why now? Who is this guy anyway? Why should I trust him? Will this work? Will this work for me? How do I get started?"

Let's tackle them one by one.

What is this book all about?

This book will help you discover your purpose and your reason for being here in life if you haven't already done so. This book also will help you discover your passion, your flow, and your superpower, inshaAllah. Once you know your purpose and passion, I will help you discover how you can combine these two and serve your Creator by serving people.

If you are sincere in your intention and persistent in your actions in implementing these steps, Allah (SWT) will grant you so much prosperity and blessing that you will thrive instead of survive, inshaAllah.

You will be and act as the main hero in your life story instead of following someone else's life. You will love what you do. You will love your life even with all of its problems. Your life will never be the same again, inshaAllah.

In a nutshell, this book is about helping you to become the main character in your life story. In other words, it will help you to discover your purpose and passion in life so you follow a path to prosperity - a blissful life with barakah (blessings) so you serve Allah (SWT) in the best way by serving others.

I could keep saying you will be thriving instead of surviving, you will be the main hero in your own story, and you will be in a state of flow, on and on. Instead, let me share a story that will paint this picture more clearly.

Story of 3 Builders

Once upon a time, a traveler was passing by a building. He saw three builders doing the same thing: laying a brick on a wall.

The traveler passes by the first builder and asks him "How is life?

What are you doing?" Builder 1 replies: "Man, life is tough. Look at what I am doing! Laying a brick. This job sucks. It doesn't pay well. Life is unfair. I wish I was resting on a beach right now."

The traveler continues and passes by the second builder and asks the same question: "How is life? What are you doing?" Builder 2 replies: "It is ok. We are building a mosque." Then he continues his work.

The traveler continues and passes by the third builder and asks the same question: "How is life? What are you building?" Builder 3 replies: "Life is beautiful. I am part of this beautiful and amazing building project. I love building. We are building a house of Allah SWT where hundreds and maybe thousands of people come and pray every day. I hope My Lord will reward me as long as this masjid is standing because I am helping to seek His pleasure. I'm so blessed, alhamdulillah. You know what? You may not believe this, but even though I offered my help free of charge, these people are paying me as well. Can you believe it?"

Even though each of the three builders is doing the same thing and even getting paid the same, their attitude and how they perceive the world and their work is different. Do you know why?

Why is the answer. More specifically, those who know *why* they do what they do is the answer we are seeking.

Most people are similar to Builder 1. They don't know why, how, or what they do. They work because they have to. They complain. They wish they didn't work at all.

Some people are similar to Builder 2. They know what and how they do what they do. They may be climbing on their career ladder. But unless they discover their "why", they are missing out on a lot in life, and may not even realize it.

Then we have Builder 3. People like Builder 3 are very rare, unfortunately, and include around 1% of people or maybe even less. They know not only what or how, but they know *why* they do what they do. They know their purpose in life. They know their passion. They turn their purpose and passion into prosperity by solving problems for people. They live their lives in awareness of Allah (SWT). Every step they take and every move they make is for Allah (SWT). They are the main heroes in their own stories. They are writing their life stories on one project, one page, one day at a time. They are preparing something beautiful for their Lord. They are pleased with their Lord in both good times and bad, by continually showing either gratefulness (*shukr*) or patience (*sabr*). Their Lord is pleased with them and grants them the best in this life and the next. They are the successful ones.

Which builder do you want to be?

Why did I write this book?

Now, let me tell you another story: mine. I was born in Uzbekistan, where Imam Al Bukhari is from. I lived there for the first 20 years of my life.

When I was 20, I traveled to Denmark to study. I had only $7 in my pocket.

For the next 10 years, I chased the things of this world (*dunya*). Alhamdulillah, I established a family with three kids. I got a house and a car. It seemed I had everything. Yet something, or rather Someone, was missing in my life.

For the last 10 years, I have been doing my best to fill that gap and to start listening and responding to my soul's longing for God. That same longing is within each one of us.

I realized that for the first part of my life, all the books, movies, and media that I consumed had all made Allah (SWT) seem irrelevant, far away, and separate from everyday life.

In the last 10 years, I have talked to thousands of Muslim entrepreneurs, professionals, and community members from all walks of life. I noticed a similar pattern. They all read similar books and watched similar movies and media. They also felt a big void in their lives, just the way I did.

Even though we are Muslims, alhamdulillah, somehow somewhere we started to "believe" the secular stories and suggestions in these books, movies, and media that tell us that Allah (SWT) is not part of, or relevant to, our success. Some of us willingly and sometimes subconsciously start to limit our awareness of Allah (SWT). We only remember Allah when we go to the masjid, or in similar cases. I was one of them, unfortunately.

What we say in our prayers doesn't match what we do in life.

Not Business, but Busyness with Allah

Life is made of 3 big parts:

- 1/3 is sleep;
- 1/3 is social life - a tiny portion of this we use for prayers;
- 1/3 is study or work.

We often think that the last third (study or work) is about us, and we view it as strictly related to business or worldly achievement. **But until we turn this business into busyness with Allah, we will never fill that void. We will never find peace.**

Surely in the remembrance of Allah do hearts find peace.
Quran, 13:28

Because, if we fill this gap with anything or anyone but Allah, our souls will never truly feel satisfied. This is because Allah (SWT) created us to know, serve, and love Him. This is what we also promised, submitted, and surrendered to when we said: "There is no god (nothing or no one worthy of placing in the center of my life) except Allah."

In the last 10 years, I have done my best to solve this problem by trying to turn to Allah and by doing my part to put that into real, practical action. In doing so, I discovered valuable approaches to life and business that I began to share with other Muslim entrepreneurs and professionals. I want to share those same steps with you, which is why I wrote this book.

One thing I can promise is this: once you dive deep into your inward journey and discover your purpose and passion, your life will never be the same again. You will have clarity of purpose and a sense of meaning. I want to guide you about how to channel this purpose and passion into a product or service that helps others, as part of your ultimate service (*'ibadah*) to Allah (SWT).

You will be the main hero in your life movie. It will be an adventure of a lifetime.

If you are what I call a "Deenpreneur" (a Muslim entrepreneur), this book will help you obtain clarity about your purpose, and discover your passion - your superpower. This will lead you to the path of prosperity.

If you are what I call a "DeenPro" (a Muslim professional), this book will help you learn principles that allow you to add more value to whatever space you work in, making you a better team player and employee. This will naturally open the path for you to climb your career ladder, obtain a raise, and have a greater positive impact.

This is what this book is all about. I hope you will enjoy this journey with me while I share my story and the story of the startups I am helping.

Step-by-Step Guide

Though I've been fortunate to connect with thousands of Muslim entrepreneurs and professionals, I often felt like there was not enough time to truly explain where they needed to focus on their journeys. Many were not ready with marketing, so I would tell them to focus on that and then come back. Others needed to make their mission or vision more focused. For many years, I wished that I could point them to one place where they could follow a clear set of steps that would prepare them for the level of success they desired.

This is the book that will guide them, and you, on that journey, inshaAllah.

False Experts

Last but not least, our Muslim community has seen enough false experts and entrepreneurs claiming big promises in 30 days or less by using Allah's name in vain.

They take their money and they are gone. Even if they offer something, it is usually one tactic and one idea to get rich quickly. For example: how to be a six-figure Muslim coach in 30 days; how to launch your Muslim E-comm Empire on Amazon, Shopify dropshipping in X days. The list goes on.

After building some companies and failing others, I learned that building a business is not easy. It takes years, not days or even months. If you are looking for a quick fix, this is not it.

What you will find are proven core pillars of building a business from Product, Promotion, Purchase, and Promise Delivery to Prosperity only after Purpose and Passion. As Muslims, we need to look into everything, even business, from both a short-term (*dunya*) and long-term (*akhirah*) lens. So hopefully, we will not be only in business, but busyness with Allah SWT which is our ultimate goal in life.

Why should you care or bother reading this?

Are you perfectly happy with where you are in life? Are you enjoying life to its fullest extent? Are you getting all the things in life you want? What do you want in this world?

Most people have no real idea what they want. They chase one shiny object after another. They escape reality. One day death will reach them. Puff. They are gone.

This book will help you answer those questions, determine what you really want, and help you figure out how to live your life to the fullest as a Muslim without compromising your Deen to Dunya.

Why now?

There is no time like now. Now is the only time you have. Because there is no guarantee of how long you live. It may sound dramatic, but you know it is true.

This book will be one of the most impactful books you will ever read because it is about you, your life's purpose, and your journey. Tomorrow may never come.

So start today.

Even if one chapter. Even if one page. Keep reading.

Who is this guy?

The reason why I ask this question is for you to know who I am and what I've done so that you can justify your time here. I understand how valuable your time is, which is why I am responding in this way. Some may think I am bragging. But this is not my intention. Allah (SWT) is the All-Knowing.

First, you can check out my profile on LinkedIn here:

https://www.linkedin.com/in/marufyusuf/

For those who are reading this book on paper, here is the overview:

- Award Winning Muslim Serial Entrepreneur (Halal.Ad, Ali Huda, Quran Era)
- Multi-Millionaire—at least on paper ⚫
- Investor & Strategy Advisor (Sakeenah, Halal Meals, Marhaba)
- Certified Life & Business Coach by Tony Robbins
- Co-founder of Halal.Ad - world-leading Muslim Marketing Agency that has served Zaytuna College and Sh. Hamza Yusuf, Zakir Naik, Bilal Philips, Suhaib Webb, Wahed Invest, UNHCR, Islamic Relief, Modanisa, Islamic Finder, Zabihah, Launch Good, MIHAS, HMC UK, Ali Huda, Quran Era, Majestic Quran, Quran Majeed App, Halal Expo Canada, Zakat Foundation and so many other Muslim scholars, companies, and startups. See a more extensive clientele list here: **www.halal.ad**

Along with the Halal.Ad team, I have also personally advised hundreds of companies and startups, most of which serve in the Muslim economy space, alhamdulillah. I also interviewed some of my fellow Muslim leaders and entrepreneurs and will be sharing some of their stories in the coming chapters, inshaAllah.

Why should you trust me?

Don't trust me. Not yet, at least. All I ask is that you read and try Step 1. If it works, then try Step 2. Then Step 3. You get the point.

Trust is built over time. Slowly. Step by step.

Will this work?

Yes. Not because I wrote this book. But because it is based on timeless wisdom in the Quran and Sunnah/Hadith. These approaches also align with tried and proven business ideas and principles that have helped thousands of successful companies.

Will this work for you?

Yes, it will, as long as you have a sincere intention backed by your consistent actions in the path of Allah, inshaAllah.

Who is this book for?

This book is for **Deenpreneurs** - Muslim entrepreneurs who are not in it just for the money but who want to serve their Creator by serving His creation to live a fulfilling life.

This book is for **Muslim Wantrepreneurs** - Muslims who aspire to be entrepreneurs, especially those who have not realized this ambition yet.

This book is for **Muslim Business Owners** who already run a business and want to take their business to the next level, inshaAllah.

This book is also for **Muslim Startups** who are looking for funds to grow their business.

This book is for **Muslim Students** who want to do something meaningful but are not sure yet which path to take in their life.

This book is for **Muslim Professionals** who want to be a part of a company that is making the world a better place, but feel stuck in their day-to-day jobs and corporate career ladder and don't know how to move forward.

We can go on and on. But to make it simple, you can test if this book is for you or not by answering these questions:

Do you love what you do? By that I mean: Is what you do something that doesn't feel like work, and you can do it for hours and hours? Do you help others with what you do to improve their lives so much that you feel a sense of fulfillment and joy? Do you make a good living out of what you do? If you answered yes to all of these questions, then congratulations! You don't need to read this book. You belong to the top 1%.

On the other hand, for the rest 99% who are on the way, this book will be very helpful, inshaAllah.

This book will help you discover your purpose and follow your passion to live in prosperity without sacrificing your deen to dunya, inshaAllah. This book also will help you to discover your story and become the main hero in your life journey.

This book also will help you get to know yourself better so you can get to know Allah SWT better.

Know that the key to knowing God is to know your own self.
—Imam Al Ghazali (May Allah have mercy on him)

This book also will help you to discover your superpowers so that you can serve God by serving others in the best way.

Who is this book NOT for?

This book is not for those who seek get-rich-quick schemes. I'm not promising a 7-figure income or salary in seven days! It is not that type of book, for that type of person.

This book requires reading, understanding, and implementing the steps as we go along.

InshaAllah, it will work. The principles I share in this book are based on tried and tested practice.

How do you get started?

The only way to start is with a sincere intention that you will commit on this path to serve Allah (SWT) and Him only.

I will present seven chapters, beginning with Purpose and Passion and leading to Prosperity.

Each chapter has some reading as well as action steps. If you want to get the most out of this book, you will need to complete the action steps as well. I promise it will change your life, inshaAllah.

Are you ready? Let's get started.

Bismillah

This journey may seem long and filled with problems. I remember the wise words of Sh. Muhammad Alshareef about problems, duas and Allah SWT.

Dua is not telling Allah about your problems.
It is telling your problems who Allah is!
Dua is an action too!
—Sh. Muhammad Alshareef

So, let's start our journey in the name of God, the One, who is The Responding One (*Al-Mujeeb*):

O Allah! Please, open our hearts, open our minds, and guide us so we will discover for what reason You created us, so we will discover what special gifts and superpowers You have granted us, so we will use these gifts to serve You and You alone. Grant us prosperity and *barakah* from You in our lives so abundantly that it will flow over our hands so that we can not only help ourselves and our families but keep giving to those in need and the orphans as well, however, do not allow the love of money to ever reach our hearts.

O, Allah! You have given us the best gift - the gift of life - witnessing all around and getting to know You and eventually loving You. While our good deeds will never be enough to enter Your garden, we will ask for Your mercy since You are The Most Merciful.

O, Allah! Guide us so that we will live our lives as you want us to live so every step we take, and every move we make will be counted as our *'ibadah*/service/worship to You—so our whole lives will be our gift to You to bring on the Last Day. Ameen!

`PURPOSE`

STEP 1 ~ PURPOSE

We did not create the heavens and the earth and everything in between without purpose.
Quran 21:16

If I ask you a simple question "How is life?", what would your answer be? Usually, there tend to be two different types of answers. Some of you say, "Life is tough. Life is unfair. Life is cruel." Others say, "Life is beautiful. Life is amazing. Life is the best gift."

Most of the time, the only difference between these groups of people is that the second group discovered their purpose in life and lived it.

"He who has a why to live for can bear with almost any how."
– Nietzsche

I have been on both ends. Growing up, life was tough. Later on, I studied and got a job. Life got easier in a materialistic sense. However, until I found out my why and followed that path, I was not truly experiencing life to the fullest.

Have you ever wondered?

Have you ever wondered: Who am I? Why am I here? What's the purpose of life? What am I supposed to do here? Is there a life after death? Why is there so much suffering in this world?

The two most important days in your life are the day you are born and the day you find out why.
— Mark Twain

In this book, I will share my journey of how I discovered answers to these questions. Hopefully, you will benefit, inshaAllah.

I could have written this book in a way that proclaims, "This is the Truth. It's my way or the highway!" But as I get older, I realize that we humans are not rational but rather emotional beings.

Universe is the greatest love poem ever being written…
What verse are you? What metaphor are you?
What do you mean?
— Amir Sulaiman

With that in mind, I have decided to write this book as if I am talking to a friend sharing my story instead of preaching. That's how I'm most comfortable connecting with others anyway. So there will be more questions than answers. There will be dialogues. You are welcome to question everything you read on these pages. If you come across a better answer, please, share it with me.

Thank you for being here. Thank you for being open-minded and open-hearted.

Another rags-to-riches story?

I also could have framed this as a rags-to-riches story about yet another multi-millionaire (at least on paper). But it would be misleading. Now that I am in my 40s and looking back and connecting the dots, I clearly see The Guide guiding me all along the way, alhamdulillah.

So, in a way, this is His story—the one that Allah SWT wrote and that I am grateful to be a part of. That's why I'm so excited about the story He is writing in your life too.

Now, let's go back to the questions. Asking those questions mentioned above would be a luxury when I was growing up. I had more pressing matters, such as finding food to eat to survive daily life.

You see, I was born in 1983 in a small city called Qarshi in the southern part of Uzbekistan. For those who don't know where this country is (trust me, many people don't), it is in Central Asia where you find lots of other countries ending in "-istan." When I usually say I am from Uzbekistan, people usually confuse it with Pakistan which is totally another country.

Positioning

Depending on whom I am talking to, I came up with a different way to introduce my country. If they are Muslims, I say I am from the country of Imam al-Bukhari and Imam al-Tirmidhi. Alhamdulillah, these scholars are very well-known among Muslims. The hadith collection Sahih Bukhari is the second most popular and authentic book after the Quran.

If they are non-Muslims, I say I am from the country of al-Khorazmi—the guy who invented Algebra, and even the word algorithm is based on his name. Do you see what I did there? I will share more about this when we talk about Promotion and Marketing in Chapter 4. For now, just remember: redefine the situation you are in,

STEP 1 ~ PURPOSE

just like I do when it comes to overcoming the hurdle of explaining where I'm from. Instead of feeling inferior and confused when you're in a situation outside of your comfort zone, try to find a positive side and an advantage. Trust me, there is always at least one!

Bitter or Better?

Why was it a luxury for me to ask questions while growing up? Simply put, I had more existential questions to deal with. Often that question was just: How do I find food to eat today?

You see, I was raised in a single-parent family. It seems that our father left us for another family. My mom (may Allah (SWT) give her the best in both worlds) raised my sister and me on her own. My maternal grandmother also lived with us. My mom was a dressmaker and she did her best to provide for the family.

Bitter to Better

I clearly remember feeling that I didn't have a father growing up. I watched my childhood friends get bikes, chocolates, gums, and many other cool things I wished I could have as a young boy, while our family barely survived. My mom did her best, but she could provide only for the basic needs of the family such as bread and milk. I wondered about our situation and wished that I could do something about it.

Now looking back, I can see that this experience was one of those deciding moments in life. I could have cursed and blamed life, or fate, or even questioned God. But I said, "Ok, I don't have a father. It means I have to figure out how to get those things on my own if I want those things." If you ask me why I took the path of responsibility instead of victimhood and blaming life, fate, or God, I don't know what to say except, "The Guide guided me."

We all struggle, and those struggles become our defining moments. In the end, it is your attitude that determines the decisions you will make. Your story includes challenges, problems, and calamities just like mine did. Ultimately, you can decide to be bitter or better. The choice is yours.

Cockroach Theory

Here is a story from Sundar Pichai - CEO of Google - on this point.

At a restaurant, a cockroach suddenly flew from somewhere and sat on a lady. She started screaming out of fear. With a panic stricken face and trembling voice, she started jumping, with both her hands desperately trying to get rid of the cockroach. Her reaction was contagious, as everyone in her group also got panicky. The lady finally managed to push the cockroach away but it landed on another lady in the group. Now, it was the turn of the other lady in the group to continue the drama. The waiter rushed forward to their rescue.

In the relay of throwing, the cockroach next fell upon the waiter. The waiter stood firm, composed himself and observed the behavior of the cockroach on his shirt. When he was confident enough, he grabbed it with his fingers and threw it out of the restaurant. Sipping my coffee and watching the amusement, the antenna of my mind picked up a few thoughts and started wondering, was the cockroach responsible for their histrionic behavior? If so, then why was the waiter not disturbed?

He handled it near to perfection, without any chaos. It is not the cockroach, but the inability of the ladies to handle the disturbance caused by the cockroach that disturbed the ladies.

I realized that, it is not the shouting of my father or my boss or my wife that disturbs me, but it's my inability to handle the disturbances caused by their shouting that disturbs me.

It's not the traffic jams on the road that disturbs me, but my inability to handle the disturbance caused by the traffic jam that disturbs me. More than the problem, it's my reaction to the problem that creates chaos in my life.

Lessons learnt from the story:

1. I understood, I should not react in life.
2. I should always respond.
3. The women reacted, whereas the waiter responded.

Reactions are always instinctive, whereas responses are always well thought of, just and right to save a situation from going out of hands, to avoid cracks in relationship, to avoid taking decisions in anger, anxiety, stress or hurry. A beautiful way to understand...........LIFE."

The HAPPY person is not because Everything is RIGHT in his Life.
He is HAPPY because his Attitude towards Everything in his Life is Right!

How could I do otherwise!?

Here is another story of twin brothers who were raised by an alcoholic father. One grew up to be an alcoholic. When asked what happened, he said, "Have you seen my father? How could I do otherwise!?"

The other grew up and never drank in his life. When he was asked what happened he said "Have you seen my father? How could I do otherwise!?" Two boys, the same dad, two different perspectives.

Your perspective in life will determine your destination. Below you will find yet another story about our inner dialogue, mindfulness and making the right choices.

The Wolf You Feed

One evening an old Cherokee told his grandson about a battle that goes on inside people.

He said, "My son, the battle is between two "wolves" inside us all.

One is Evil. It is anger, envy, jealousy, sorrow, regret, greed, arrogance, self-pity, guilt, resentment, inferiority, lies, false pride, superiority, and ego.

The other is good. It is joy, peace, love, hope, serenity, humility, kindness, benevolence, empathy, generosity, truth, compassion and faith."

The grandson thought about it for a minute and then asked his grandfather: "Which wolf wins?"

The old Cherokee simply replied, "The one you feed."

Balloon Entrepreneur at age 7

Necessity is the mother of all inventions.
—Proverb

I soon realized that to achieve what my friends had, I needed to take matters into my own hands. I knew there was no one else who could do it for me. With that in mind, I asked myself, "How can I get my hands on some candies, gum, balloons, and other cool stuff?" I also knew that whatever I did had to be enjoyable for me, not just a means to make money. I was, after all, just a child.

By some stroke of luck, I obtained one som (Uzbekistan's national currency whose value has since significantly decreased). I was only seven years old at the time. I lived near an old bazaar where thousands of people walked by our streets every day. I had enough foot traffic; all I needed was something to offer them.

I went to the wholesale bazaar, which was much further away but offered much cheaper prices. After searching, I found a set of 100 balloons that caught my attention, so I bought it and headed home.

Upon arrival, I hung the balloon set on a metal bar that was part of the gas distribution system on every street. I had set up my booth, and the fascinating thing about this set was that it had a large balloon in the center. When someone bought a balloon, they could choose a number to win the big one. If they chose the right number, they would receive a huge balloon, but if not, they would still get another balloon from the set.

After doing some research, I discovered that the average balloon price was around one som. I was taken aback by the price difference

between wholesale and retail, but it was a pleasant surprise. So, I set the price at one som per balloon and did some quick calculations. To my delight, I realized that if I sold all of my balloons, I would earn 100 soms, despite only spending one som.

I couldn't believe it! I was eager to begin selling.

At age 7

My first customers

As soon as I hung up my balloon set, my friends from the street gathered around my booth. All I did was explain how it works, and how they could win the big balloon. The game had started. My friends ran home and begged their moms and dads to win the big balloon.

Building on One Idea

In a mere matter of days, I had sold all of my balloons. I did earn 100 soms. Suddenly, I could afford chewing gums, candies, and whatever I thought was cool at that age just like everyone else. I couldn't believe it at first. It felt like a true miracle. But as I sold more and more balloons, I became more and more confident. I realized that earning enough money for our family to be able to afford extra things was a real possibility. As I was busy selling the balloons, another idea came. Why not sell chewing gum and candies to my customer friends? I knew their parents were already buying these from somewhere every day. Why wouldn't they buy from me?

Guess what I started selling next? :)

My First Employee

In September, summer ended and I had to go to school. Of course, when I was at school, no one would attend my booth, so no sales. After some thought, I asked my mom (the central figure in my 7-year-old social network) if she could attend my booth while I was gone. She agreed. From that day on, I would rush home and ask about how much we sold. Suddenly, I was making money even when I was learning at school. Without even knowing, it seems that I hired my own mother as my first employee!

Catch Me if You Can

As I reflected on my situation, I also realized that my only way out from my city to a larger world was education. This led me to study hard at school. The more I learned, the more I got curious about the things I learned about. In first grade, they teach the alphabet for six months. I asked my grandmother if she could teach me the letters and she did (she was my first teacher - may Allah (SWT) grant her *Jannat al Firdaws*). In a week or so, I learned all the letters and how to join them so I could read words. I enjoyed it so much that I started and finished the alphabet book we were supposed to complete in six months in only one month.

From that moment, I did the same with other subjects, such as math and others. Alhamdulillah, I started getting straight A's. Soon my class teachers and other teachers at school started noticing. They started giving me extra homework. Since I already did my class homework, this extra work was not a big deal to me.

When I was in 5th grade, I became easily bored in class since I had already read and completed the books in advance. The school noticed and moved me from the second half of 5th grade to the second half of 6th grade. I had to catch up on a year's worth of work, and I did. Later, they moved me again from the second half of 7th grade to the second half of 8th grade.

Believe it or not, I was on my way to finishing high school at the very young age of 12. But then something happened in the summer of 1996.

At this point, you might be thinking, "OK, Maruf was a straight-A student. But I wasn't." Bear with me—the point I am trying to share has very little to do with straight As.

Consider the 2002 movie "Catch Me If You Can." At one point, the film's main character Frank teaches as a professor at a university even though he never studied that subject. Later on, when the FBI interviews him and asks about this, he simply says that he only read one chapter ahead.

The lesson is: if you are proactive and do a bit more than others, you will go further faster. Now back to the story.

Crushing my Ego

In the summer of 1996, a friend told me that there was a new boys-only boarding school in town. The high school was known as the

Uzbek Turk Anadolu Lisesi, and all subjects were only taught in English.

The school was inviting students to come to take exams. I followed my friend there and took the exam. I found the exam very strange and intriguing. It didn't assess any of the knowledge I had learned in school but was instead a set of questions that didn't require predefined knowledge. Later I found out that they were logical questions to find out my IQ.

After a week or so, the results came back. My score was one of the top three scores among the thousands of students who had participated. I was very surprised and happy. I knew I had made my mother and grandmother proud. But now I had to make a tough decision.

If I stayed in my public school, I was on my way to graduating with honors and being one of the youngest in the whole country to do so. If I switched to this Turkish high school, I would lose all this progress and join my classmates at the same age and the same grade.

Little did I know that making these types of decisions would later become a recurring event in my life.

After giving it some thought, I knew that mastering English could help me in my future education and career. I also considered that if this new school's exams were different, their teaching must be different as well. I ultimately decided to go with the Turkish gymnasium.

Oh, boy! What a difference! The school started in September. I went in thinking that I was at the top. Soon I realized that I was at the bottom of the class. You see, at this new school, they mainly taught English for 20 hours every week for the first year. It was called the Preparation class. While my English was considered good at the public school, I in fact barely knew only a few words, such as "apple," "red," "table," and the like.

For my first year, Mr. Selim Vural was my English teacher. He was one of the first truly passionate teachers that I witnessed in my life. One of the most admirable things about him was his passion to teach English not only to skilled students but also to struggling students as well, which is much more challenging.

At the end of each week, he would test all of us. The test would show each of us where we were. Lo and behold, I was at the bottom. It crushed my ego. One moment I was seemingly at the top, and the next I was at the bottom of the class getting low marks on tests.

Turkish High School class photo. Mr. Vural is sitting in the first front row. Can you find me in this photo?

At this moment, I could have gone back to my old school where I was at the top. But I knew deep in my heart it was not the right path. Instead, I decided to stay and take on this challenge as a game. I had to get better every week, even if just by one point on the test.

Because it was a boarding school, my classmates from outside the city could stay in the dormitory while the students from the city could go home. Most of my city classmates went back home every day. But I decided to stay.

First, I thought it would be fun for me to spend time with my classmates outside school as well. Most of them were smarter than me. I knew I could learn a thing or two. I knew they studied together, so I joined them.

Secondly, I would save so much time by avoiding the traffic involved in going home and coming back.

Last, but not the least, I would also save my family my travel costs and daily food. So I only visited my family during the weekends.

Dorm life was fun. My new friends and I played soccer and basketball together, but we also studied hard. As we spent day and night together, over the years we developed an extremely strong bond of friendship. I am still friends and in touch with most of them from that period until now, alhamdulillah.

Staying at the dorm with smarter friends and studying hard started showing results. I started climbing up the ranks in our weekly English tests. By the end of that first year, I would be among the best in the class, alhamdulillah. Even Mr. Vural would ask me and other top students to teach and help some of our classmates.

Looking back, I can now connect the dots and see how pivotal that first year, my teachers, my friends at the dorm, and the whole environment at the Turkish gymnasium were in my life journey. The whole experience, especially embracing English, opened many new doors in the future. Even this book you are holding now would not be a possibility if it weren't for that experience.

Peer Pressure

My next target was the university. Everyone was trying to enroll in the most popular and prestigious one: The University of World Economy and Diplomacy. I said to myself: "This is where I am going then."

Now the competition was even higher. You had to aim to be among the top 1,000 students in the country, otherwise, you had to pay an arm and a leg to attend, which I simply couldn't afford.

There was only one problem.

Mastering Math

To enroll in this university, students had to master English, Uzbek, and Math. While I was good in English and Uzbek, I had to master math which I didn't like. At least, I didn't like how it was taught to me at that time.

Yet another teacher, Ulugbek Ustaz (Ustaz means master or teacher in Uzbek), introduced me to Advanced Math and Geometry on another level. I started finally understanding and slowly began to like and eventually love math. Unfortunately, he passed away suddenly in his 40s which was a great loss for our community. May Allah grant him the best in the next life.

What I learned from my time with him is that you can learn anything. Right now, you may have subjects you were not good at and hated at school. If you had a great teacher who could actually teach you that subject with passion, you would be hooked. Because there is really no boring subject, especially at school. It just takes the right teacher to illuminate that subject and bring it to life.

What's Best for Others May Not Be Best for You

After mastering math, Allah (SWT) graced me with admission into the most prestigious university in Uzbekistan. I started learning about the International Economy.

But soon I found out that what is best for others may not be the best for me. Learning about the economy was too much theory for me. Besides, I couldn't see myself using this knowledge after my graduation in a newly independent Uzbekistan. My country had been ruled under a planned economy, rather than a market economy, with tremendous corruption during the last 100-year reign of the Soviet Union. I was interested in other things.

Love at First Sight

I showed up to class mainly to make an appearance, but the class ended up being the place where I was introduced to personal computers for the first time. Don't get me wrong—we had computers at boarding school. But we had almost no access. Computer classes were mainly about some gibberish commands on a blue screen to copy and paste files from one location to another without really knowing why.

While in university, I suddenly had access to Pentium III computers with colorful displays where you could drag and drop. I was hooked. It was love at first sight.

I knew I had to get one of these. But how? One of my roommates knew how to assemble computers. I started offering that service to my fellow students; I was no stranger to hard work and earning an income in creative ways. Soon, we found a few students who needed help setting up their computers. After setting up just two or three computers, I had saved up enough to buy one for myself.

As soon as I had my hands on the computer, I started clicking and checking out each application on it, and following each link and where it leads. Meanwhile, I was thinking about how I could make a living out of this field.

There were many assignments from the university. Each student had to prepare short papers on different topics. The students had to type those on the computers and print them out. They had to cross the street to print them out. It was a bit of a burden.

Just like my childhood balloon shop, I soon realized that all I needed was to buy a printer to make my dorm into a print shop! I got a printer and just like that, my investment started paying off. My service soon got so much demand that students wanted to use my printing services 24/7. I had to hire my roommate so he could take care of it when I couldn't.

I knew then that computers were the future. I told myself that I had to do something with this. I didn't know what exactly yet. I also knew that Uzbekistan was way behind in Information Technology. If I really want to learn and master this, I had to go abroad. My first goal was to go to America. For whatever reason, it never really worked out. It was not written for me.

Deciding on Denmark

One day a friend suggested that interviews were being held for students to receive full scholarships to study in Denmark. The program was related to computers, especially multimedia design. I said to myself, "Why not?"

My strategy was simple, straightforward, and honest. I said in the interview with full confidence: "Thank you for this opportunity. I admit I don't know much about computers. I recently got one and I am obsessed with it. I really want to learn IT. I realize that I need to go abroad to do this. If you give me this chance, I will do my best to study Multimedia Design." I got a call after a few days that I was granted the full scholarship.

Now I had to make another decision.

Was I willing to leave the most prestigious university in Uzbekistan and let go of two years of study, to start over at a college in Denmark? By now, it was clear to me which way to go. I knew going abroad was the only way to advance in my desired field of computers and technology. Still, many of my friends told me I was crazy to drop out of the university which was a dream place to study for hundreds of thousands of people.

On January 20th, 2003, I landed in Denmark with $7 in my pocket. I spent all the money I had to buy a one-way ticket to Denmark. On one hand, I had tremendous joy. I felt like I had made it. I was finally abroad where I could learn what I loved. On the other hand, I only had $7 and knew I had to find a job to survive.

It was a mixed feeling. Somehow, overall I felt good, alhamdulillah.

Looking back, I don't know what I was thinking. How could I relocate to another country with only $7 in hand? On the other hand, I had nothing to lose. I didn't have a wife or kids. I had to figure out how to survive in the new place.

Delivering Newspapers at 5 a.m.

Finding a job was much easier than I thought. A gentleman named Jim visited our dormitory and offered a job to deliver newspapers and earn 50 cents per delivery. I couldn't believe my ears. I did some quick math: If I could deliver 300 papers a day, I could earn $150 per day. That was a month's salary back home! I signed up for that job right there and then without much hesitation.

I soon realized I had to deliver these papers early in the morning around 5 a.m., no matter the wind, rain, or snow. Sometimes I had to go up and down four to five stories or flights of stairs just to deliver one paper. Moreover, Denmark was one of the highest tax-paying countries, and my salary was taxed at 47% or more.

But I had no other choices. It was still better than any job I could imagine back in Uzbekistan.

Over the years until I finished my studies, newspaper delivery turned into cleaning toilets, cleaning office buildings, assembling furniture, washing restaurant dishes, and so many others.

My experience is not unique. Anyone who has to establish themselves on their own goes through a similar journey. What is great about this journey is that it will teach you to be humble and grateful for what you already have. During those times, the only thing that kept me going was that it was temporary. I kept my sights set on my goal: I would finish my studies and finally get a job I would like, inshaAllah.

Climbing The Career Ladder

Finally, that day came. I got a web designer position in a small web design agency. I started designing beautiful web pages that would be delivered to the client, and then we would move on. But I began to notice that most of these sites were not visited often. I started learning web analytics, information architecture, search engine optimization, marketing, and whatever I could find to learn not only how to make websites look good, but to make them useful to many people.

Over the next 10 years, I changed companies every two to three years in order to take on an even bigger challenge. I was advancing and climbing my career ladder fast.

My last corporate job was at Vestas, the world's largest wind turbine manufacturer, where I was a part of the team responsible for the intranet and website. The job was great. The team was great. The salary was great.

By that time, I got married and had two beautiful children. I had a house and a car. It seems that I had finally checked all the items on Maslow's Hierarchy of Needs. I was, by many standards, a "success."

Yet something, or more accurately Someone, was missing. Later I found out that Maslow wrote one more step on his pyramid which is called Transcendence but never published it. I won't describe this here because I feel I have found an even better module that is Allah-centric, but it is worth looking into.

Identity Crisis

Parallel to climbing the career ladder, I had been asking myself the same existential questions shared at the beginning of this chapter. Who am I? Why am I here? What is the purpose of life? In the beginning, it was from time to time. The more time passed, the more frequently I keep asking these questions.

Just to give you context, let me explain. I knew very little about Islam. Most of what I knew was hearsay and I probably didn't understand why I did what I did. I arrived in Denmark two years after 9/11 - September 11, 2001. Danish TV channels kept showing long-bearded guys shouting and blowing up stuff. Little did I know that it was propaganda showing only one side of the story.

On the other hand, a young man who leaves his sunshine country for cold, windy, and gloomy weather without seeing the sun for weeks at a time naturally begin to ask some existential questions. Why do I wake up every morning? What am I doing here? Who am I? Am I really a part of a religion that hates these people and blows them up? It was a classic identity crisis. I didn't know these fancy terms back then. But that's what it was.

Straight to Science

Some people believe in things without question. I am not one of them. I need to check and verify. So when I wanted to know our origin as human beings and the origin of the universe, I didn't want to go to religion but straight to science. Science at least provides some evidence, I thought.

So I started with the theory of evolution. While it explained how living things might have evolved, the theory had many missing elements. I am not going into a long debate on this. If you do a bit of research on the internet, you will find the missing parts.

I wanted to go even further, so I dived into Cosmology. That path takes us to the Big Bang. Beyond the Big Bang, it is all assumptions, even in science.

Later I would discover the Kalam cosmological argument originated by Imam Al Ghazali as the following:

- Everything that begins to exist has a cause.
- The universe began to exist.
- Therefore, the universe has a cause.

This Cause must be Powerful Creator, uncaused, outside time-space, eternal - beginningless, immaterial among other things.

"Science without religion is lame, religion without science is blind."
—*Albert Einstein*

Comparative Religion

I once read somewhere that science studies how, while religion studies why. So I started looking into different world religions. Before I dove into thousands of world religions, I established some criteria:

1. Religion must have a God because otherwise, it is just a set of man-made rules and values (even the Big Bang was started by something or by someone!).
2. Religion must have a scripture that I can read and verify to my

satisfaction.

By applying these rules, there were not many religions to examine. I was looking into Judaism, Christianity, and Islam. I thought I knew Islam so I disregarded it easily. I also noticed a pattern: one God kept sending messengers with a similar message. When looking into Judaism, I found out that I can't join simply because it is complicated or you must ethnically be a Jew. I thought to myself "If there is a God, that God must be just. Judaism can't be a global religion since I have no control over which race I am born. It is not fair or just." So, Judaism was not a choice for me.

Second, I looked into Christianity. I read the Bible. I liked many of the teachings and stories. However, I was really surprised how prophets - special people God chose - could do such sins as sleeping with their own daughters, etc. Moreover, since I was exposed to One God in Islam, I couldn't understand or accept Trinity. It just didn't make sense to me.

When it came to Islam, as I said before, I thought I knew it. It is ironic that when you know very little, you think you know so much. Besides, Soviet propaganda about Islam as a backward religion in Uzbekistan really worked well on our people, including me.

I thought I was at a dead end. I almost gave up. And then I came across an e-book entitled "Scientific Miracles in the Quran."

Quran Rediscovered

This book describes the scientific miracles in the Quran such as the expanding universe, the rotation of the planets, the development of the human embryo, and so much more. I started cross-checking each claim in the Quran with English translation. It was right there.

Then it hit me.

I had actually never read the Quran with the proper translation and understanding until then. I assumed it was an old book with some stories and commandments on how to behave. It began to seem to me that it was perhaps more than that. So I picked up the Quran and started reading, to understand.

I was reading the Quran to answer my questions. The first one was...

So Why Are We Here?

My first question was: Why am I here on this planet? What is my purpose? This is what I found in the Quran:

> *I (Allah) did not create jinn and humans except to worship Me.*
> *Quran, 51:56*

When I read or hear the word worship, the only thing that comes to my mind is someone performing salah - the five daily prayers or prostrating in *sajdah*. I thought, "If this is the only reason for human creation, then we are failing greatly at that!" Then I came across "Even Angels Ask," a book authored by an American convert to Islam and math professor Dr. Jeffrey Lang. He asks similar questions in his book and explains that even the angels would ask Allah SWT in the Quran about the purpose of man's existence.

> *'Remember' when your Lord said to the angels, "I am going to place a successive 'human' representative on earth." They asked 'Allah', "Will You place in it someone who will spread corruption there and shed blood while we glorify Your praises and proclaim Your holiness?" Allah responded, "I know what you do not know."*
> *Quran, 2:30*

From Worship to Service

Later I would discover that the same Arabic word, '*ibadah*, expands in meaning from not only worship but to serve God as well. I also would find out that Allah doesn't need any serving or my prayers. As humans, we serve Allah (SWT) by serving His creation as His representative on Earth.

The way we serve is to show mercy because we are the servant of The Most Merciful. We act kindly because we are the servant of the Most Kind. We act justly because we are the servant of The Most Just. This service would include not only our five daily prayers or remembrance of God (*dhikr*), but any action done with a sincere intention to please Him and serve Him and Him alone.

> *The Prophet (SAW) said: "When one of you has sexual intercourse with his wife, he receives the reward of sadaqah."*
>
> *They said, "O Messenger of Allah! Will he still receive the reward when he satisfies his lust?"*
>
> *He answered: "Would it not be haram if he satisfied his lust through haram ways? When he satisfies his lust through halal (legitimate) ways, he will receive rewards."*
>
> *Sahih Muslim 1006*

For example, even sleeping could be your way of serving Him if you make a sincere du'a that you are resting in order to wake up tomorrow and be able to serve Him.

> *Say, "Surely my prayer, my worship, my life, and my death are all for Allah—Lord of all worlds."*
> *Quran, 6:162*

I came to the incredible realization that true Islam—true submission to God—was about being God-conscious in every step you take and every move you make.

This totally changed how I perceived Islam. The more I learned about Islam from the sources, the more new things I discovered. I asked myself "What if I misunderstood even the basics such as the five pillars of Islam?" So I started to examine everything I knew about Islam.

There is no God but Allah?

Growing up, I used to think that if I believed (like I believe that it may rain today) that there is a God, I am good. I might decide to do some prayers later when I get old because this is what I saw in my country. To be honest, I was often told that God is free of all needs. So I thought, "He doesn't need my prayers anyway. I may do some good here and there in my life, but the rest of it I can enjoy as I want."

Then I came across a video by Shaykh Yasir Qadhi (may Allah (SWT) reward him) on YouTube where he explains the meaning of "la ilaha illa Allah." Usually, it is translated as "There is no god except Allah." But who is God? I mean, what does the word God mean? Because I knew that the Arabs of old times were wrong to worship many idols as gods, I figured that as long as I believed that one God existed, I was safe. But I was struck by how Sh. Yasir explained that the concept of god extends beyond this literal meaning into anything or anyone you put in the center of your life. The same meaning is found in the following ayah from the Quran as well:

Have you seen ˹O Prophet˺ those who have taken their own desires as their god? ˹And so˺ Allah left them to stray knowingly, sealed their hearing and hearts, and placed a cover on their sight. Who then can guide them after Allah? Will you ˹all˺ not then be mindful?
Quran, 45:23

I began to realize that a "god" could be someone or something you place in the center of your life as the main goal. It could be money. It could be fame. It could be power. It could literally be anything. When I looked into my life and examined it, I witnessed that at the center of my life was dunya - material wealth.

What is at the center of your everyday life?

Struggling to Surrender

Once I understood the true meaning of the first pillar of Islam—to submit yourself, your desires, your life, your work, and your everything to Allah and Allah alone—I experienced a period where there was internal conflict and struggle to submit.

It is like having your first child. Up until that moment, you are the center of your universe. Then after the birth of your child, he or she becomes the center of your universe. That same experience was happening again, but this time the transition was how to willingly submit myself to Allah (SWT).

One of the best things that helped me is to get to Allah (SWT) by His Beautiful Names. One of His names is Al Warith - The Inheritor. As I told myself that I needed to submit to God, I soon saw how many tricks my ego played. Remembering Allah's name Al Warith helped to reorient me. I owned nothing, really. In reality, He is the Owner. I didn't own this body. It was from Him. It will return to Him. I was temporarily renting this shell. Slowly but surely, I was surrendering bit by bit, alhamdulillah.

There is a famous saying in the Islamic tradition: "Die before you die." While it's not clear if this was originally stated by the Prophet Muhammad *(SAW)*, there is another close statement by Umar ibn al-Kttab (RA): *"Take yourself into account before you are taken into account..."* in

Muhasabat al-Nafs 2.

I bear witness that there is no god (nothing or no one to put in the center of my life) except Allah (SWT) and I bear witness that Muhammad (SAW) is His servant and messenger.

This is the statement I have been slowly and gradually embracing in the last 10 years. Maybe that's something you've struggled with, or are still struggling with, as well.

But why did it take me so long to reach that point?

Islam & Secularism

Over the last decade, I have talked to over 1,000 Muslim Entrepreneurs and Professionals one on one. The recurring theme was that they were not happy where they were in life. They wanted to live a life with meaning and purpose. At first, I thought the concern of each person was just related to their personal path in life. But then I saw a pattern that was too repetitive to ignore.

I recognized what was going on after reading the book "Islam & Secularism" by Syed Muhammad Naquib Al Attas. To understand the concept in this book, we need to go back to Europe's Dark Ages, which was the same time as the Golden Ages in Islamic civilization. During the Golden Ages, Muslim scholars and scientists were leading science and invention. "1001 Inventions" by National Geographic is a good book to look into if you are interested in more about this Muslim legacy.

For example, Muslims invented many things. Fatima Al Firhi founded the first university in 859. Muhammad Al Khwarizmi invented Algebra and even the term algorithm is based on his name. Around the year 1000 Ibn al-Haitham proved that humans see objects by light reflecting off of them and entering the eye, dismissing Euclid and Ptolemy's theories that light was emitted from the eye itself. The first hospital was the Ahmad ibn Tulun Hospital, founded in 872 in Cairo. Ibn Al Haytham (965–1039) was a polymath and he is considered to be the father of modern scientific methodology due to his emphasis on experimental data and the reproducibility of its results.

Muslim scholars and scientists saw their work as their service to Allah (SWT). They were looking into the sky and into themselves, upwards and inwards, and anywhere in between, all with wonder and hope of seeing the signs of Allah (SWT) as is encouraged in the Quran.

While in Europe, the situation was different. The church suffocated science if it was going against what the church believed. Galileo's story is a good example: his belief that the earth moved and revolved around the sun led the Catholic church to deem him a heretic. The church believed the earth did not move and was the center of the universe. From that moment on, religion and science started to go their own ways.

It was the start of secularism. Here is the definition from Wikipedia: Secularism is most commonly defined as the separation of religion from civil affairs and the state and may be broadened to a similar position seeking to remove or minimize the role of religion in any public sphere.

From the past until the present day, secularism is everywhere. They have removed God from almost any book we read, and any media we consume. Unfortunately, it has also affected how most of us understand and practice Islam. We have limited Islam to masjids or our five daily prayers—or even less.

Muslims read these secular books, watch secular movies, and listen to songs. We are building our business based on these secular ideas. We are pursuing careers based on these secular ideas of success. I know this firsthand because I experienced it myself.

While this path may or may not result in material wealth, it will not fulfill you as a human being. Why? For that, we need to look into ourselves and examine ourselves better. Who are we? Are we bodies with souls? Or are we souls with bodies?

Soul Searching

In order to practice what I preach, I wanted to really understand science-based approaches to how human beings achieve success. That's what led me to become a certified life coach by Tony Robbins. I am also a habits coach by B.J. Fogg, who holds a Ph.D. in Psychology from Stanford University. I learned so much about human psychology and why we do what we do from these programs. They helped me to create new good habits and get rid of bad ones.

However, I was still not satisfied. I realized the same thing. They did their best but God was out of the equation.

This is when I looked into Islam to see if it offered a similar approach. I came across the following Islamic Psycho-Spiritual Model by Dr. Abdallah Rothman on a Productive Muslim blog.

Whoever knows himself, knows his Lord.
Source: Hilyat al-Awliyā' 10/208

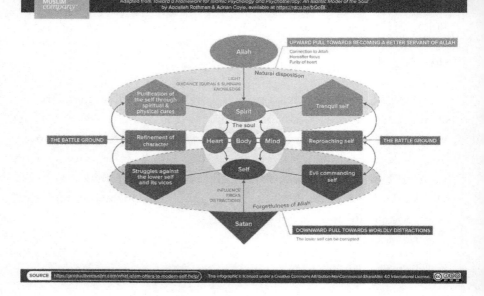

Alhamdulillah, Islam has such a huge treasure of knowledge we don't appreciate. Unfortunately, most of this is still in Arabic. Even this work is built upon the Muslim scholars of the past such as Imam al-Ghazali and others. It is also based on the Quran and Hadith. Let me share what I learned from this.

Fitrah

Basically, we as humans are in one of these two states: *Fitrah* or *Ghaflah*.

Fitrah is our natural disposition and our awake state. It is the soul's true identity. This is the state where we see reality as it is without any blinds. It should be our goal to be in this state. This is the state mentioned in the following hadith:

> *Abu Huraira reported: The Prophet (SAW) said, "No child is born but that he is upon natural instinct - fitrah. His parents make him a Jew, or a Christian, or Magian… ".*

Sahih Al-Bukhārī 1292

Ghaflah

Then there is another state: *Ghaflah*. This is the state of being spiritually asleep or involved in the forgetfulness of Allah. It is the state we keep straying to without course correcting. We don't care. We are indifferent. We don't come back to Allah. If we keep doing this consistently, Allah eventually seals our hearts, minds, eyes, and hearing. We may see the signs, but we don't realize them. There is a covering.

Allah has sealed their hearts and their hearing, and their sight is covered. They will suffer mighty punishment.
Quran, 2:7

Mindset, Bodyset, Heartset, Soulset

According to this model, we not only have a body that makes us a physical entity, but we also have a mind, heart, and soul that make us rational, emotional, and spiritual entities as well.

Recently, the term mindset became so popular that everyone seems to know what it is and how we can benefit from it. While it is true that how we think has a huge impact on our daily lives, so do the other parts.

I first heard the terms "bodyset," "heartset," and "soulset" from Canadian writer and leadership expert Robin Sharma. I think he is onto something. We should be taking care of not only our mindset (how we think), but also our bodyset (how we move), heartset (how we feel), and soulset (how we get to know the One).

Three Types of Souls

If only it were that easy to have our bodies, minds, hearts, and souls all aligned in perfect health and balance! There's just one problem: our Self (ego or *nafs*). While our soul is called the Upper Self, our lower base ego self is called the Lower Self, since it is driven by worldly desires such as food, shelter, intercourse, and other base drives.

In fact, the Qur'an and Islamic tradition describe three types of selves:

1. *Nafs al-Mutma'innah* - Content Soul at Peace
2. *Nafs al-Lawwamah* - Self-Reproaching Soul
3. *Nafs al-Ammarah* - Evil-Commanding Self

The battlegrounds of our lives are such that we will have the opportunity, and challenge, to experience and choose between these three states. When there is a covering on our hearts by Allah SWT because we don't care and are in a state of *Nafs al-Ammarah*, we manifest character qualities that are destructive, such as anger, jealousy, and envy; these are called destroyers.

When we are engaged in struggling against our lower selves (*jihad al-nafs*), attempting to reign in our lower tendencies toward individuation and self-direction, we are in a state of *Nafs al-Lawwamah*, where we take ourselves to account and make an effort to do the work of turning our hearts toward God.

The Prophet Muhammad (SAW) said, "there is a piece of flesh in the body, and when it is sound the whole body is sound, and when it is corrupt the whole body is corrupt and indeed that is the heart."
Sahih Al Bukhari

When we have moments of success in this process we can experience the soul in a state of peace and rest, the state of *Nafs al-Mutma'innah*. While it is rare to fully achieve this state, out of His mercy God provides us glimpses of it that keep us motivated to do the work of striving toward that next best version of ourselves, having more frequent experiences of that state of the soul.

Freedom

One of the takeaways from all of this for me was about true freedom. Our capitalistic society in which we live tells us that it is all about freedom. But the kind of freedom offered is the freedom of worldly desires that feels good to our lower ego selves.

Contrary to this notion, the Islamic paradigm is also about freedom— not freedom of the ego, but freedom of the soul *from* the ego. When we tame and control our egos, we free our souls. When the soul is polished and purified, it is a guiding light by Allah that will help us come closer to the Source in every step we take.

Making Sense All of These

So how do we make sense of this? After learning all of this knowledge, I just wanted to connect the dots and make meaning. The ideas we just covered are life-changing! They change your perspective and how you look at the world. They take you to a different dimension.

As Muslims, we believe that this world is a temporary place, a simulation or test. If you're a movie buff, you can call it something like a matrix.

As I considered all of this, I wanted to know if I had missed something. I went back to the origin story of human life in the Quran, which begins in Surah al-Baqara, verse 30, where Allah (SWT) says,

"I'm creating a representative on Earth." But the angels ask, "Why would you create something that sheds blood and does bad things, while we glorify your name?" Allah (SWT) says, "I know something which you do not know." Then He teaches Adam (AS) the names of things, which symbolizes knowledge. This indicates that we humans have the capacity to learn new things.

> *So when I have fashioned him and had a spirit of My Own breathed into him, fall down in prostration to him.*
> *Quran, 15:29*

Another verse in the Quran mentions that Allah (SWT) breathed out of His Spirit into Adam (AS), which is the soul that we discussed above. Then, as the story goes, Adam (AS) is given free will.

So the initial elements of man's creation are knowledge, soul, and free will. As I pondered these verses, I noticed that the real conflict emerges when Allah (SWT) asks the angels and Iblis to prostrate to Adam (AS). All of the angels do so, except Iblis, who says, "I am better than him."

Who is this human being? Who is this immensely valuable creation to whom Allah (SWT) asked all his angels to prostrate, despite the human being's shortcomings? Who is this human being that even Iblis (Satan) became an outcast for in an attempt to lead him astray?

Allah (SWT), in His ultimate wisdom, knew all the pluses and minuses of creating human beings. Yet He wanted and created us. We are here, even as the innocent angels perfectly glorify His name in His presence. Still, Allah (SWT) asked the angels to bow down to man, symbolizing he is better. So what does this really mean to us? What does this say about who we really are, in the sight of God?

Life is a Precious Gift

Let's recap. We, humans, were given the gift of life, including the capacity for knowledge, a soul, and free will.

This is a human experiment. The test of life is tough. Yes, there will be those who don't care. There will be those who are distracted by dunya - all materialistic things or destructive desires. Many will fail.

Yet against all odds even in these conditions, there will be those who sincerely want to know and get closer to their Creator and strive in His path. Those are the successful ones. Those are even better than the angels.

This is the moral of the Grand Life Story. Once you realize that, you appreciate your life. Because it is such a beautiful gift. It's such a beautiful opportunity. It's such a beautiful invitation to live up to that status, inshallah. We ask Allah (SWT) to make us among those beautiful souls. Ameen.

Islam, Iman, Ihsan

That invitation is Islam. That path is Islam. Islam is not simply a set of rules and beliefs, but also the path of constant self-improvement. Our purpose is to come closer and closer to the Creator, to become excellent servants and moral leaders, to the point that our individual will and the eternal Will of the Creator become perfectly aligned. It is the moment when we join all of creation and fulfill our created purpose. It is the moment we get into what psychologists describe as "a state of flow."

But Islam is in levels. The three levels of our deen were revealed to the Prophet Muhammad (SAW) in the famous hadith about his encounter with the Angel Gabriel (AS). Gabriel came to the Prophet (SAW) while he was surrounded by his companions and he said, "O Muhammad, tell me about Islam."

The Prophet (SAW) said: "Islam is

1. to testify that there is no true god but Allah and that Muhammad is the Messenger of Allah,
2. to establish (5 daily) prayers,
3. to give charity,
4. to fast the month of Ramadan,
5. and to perform the Hajj pilgrimage to the House if one can find a way."

Gabriel (AS) said, "You have spoken truthfully," and then he said, "Tell me about faith/iman."

The Prophet (SAW) said: "Iman is to believe in

1. Allah,
2. His angels,
3. His books,
4. His messengers,
5. the Last Day,
6. and to believe in the Divine Decree (*al-qadar*), both it's good and it's evil."

Gabriel (AS) said, "You have spoken truthfully, so tell me about excellence (Ihsan)."

The Prophet (SAW) said: "Ihsan is to worship Allah as if you see Him. Even though you do not see Him, He surely sees you."

This hadith describes our journey before us, from religious infancy to spiritual maturity: surrender (Islam), faith (Iman), and excellence (Ihsan).

Imam Ibn Taymiyyah explains the hadith, writing:

"The hadith of Gabriel clarifies that Islam is built upon five pillars, which is Islam itself. It is not based upon anything other than its foundation. Rather, the Prophet (SAW) designated three degrees of religion. The pinnacle is excellence (Ihsan), its middle is faith (Iman), and its base is Islam."

Solving for Firdaus

The Prophet (SAW) said, "… if you ask Allah for anything, ask Him for the Firdaus, for it is the last part of Paradise and the highest part of Paradise, and at its top, there is the Throne of Beneficent, and from it gush forth the rivers of Paradise."
Sahih al-Bukhari 7423

The Prophet (SAW) encourages us to ask for the best. For us to get there, we should also aim for the best: the pinnacle of our deen which is Ihsan. After all, the best reward is given for the best effort.

Imagine being one of these blessed people on the day of Judgement:

As for those given their book (of deeds) in their right hand, they will cry (happily), "Here (everyone)! Read my book! I surely knew I would face my reckoning." They will be in a life of bliss…
Quran, 69:19-21

Our journey is to Allah (SWT). Our destination is Allah (SWT). We belong to Him. Surely, our return is also to Him. We have nowhere else to go. He has also given us so much that we can't even imagine or count our blessings. What is the best gift we can present to be thankful?

We should pay close attention to this example of such a blissful life that Allah (SWT) shows us in this verse. How do we solve for that person and their book? Imagine this is your book. What would it say inside?

Do you think that there will be some good things you did here and there happening haphazardly? Or do you think this book will be about you and your beautiful life story and how you lived your life on your journey to Allah in a way that is planned with a purpose, in a way where you are the main hero?

Have you ever wondered why we love stories? Especially those stories and movies where the main hero overcomes a challenge that seems impossible. I sincerely believe it is in our fitrah– our natural disposition or DNA or whatever you call it–that we as humans are born to overcome challenges against all odds.

If we are overcoming challenges because we believe in a higher cause with meaning and we are on the right path, we feel alive and awake and in a state of flow. Not because we are powerful on our own. But because we are backed by the Most Powerful if we seek His help.

At times, it may seem too much. We hope and intend to do better. But we fail. We fail again. When we fail, we should remember the following hadith:

Aisha (RA) reported: The Messenger of Allah (SAW) said, "Follow the right course, be devoted, and give glad tidings. Verily, none of you will enter Paradise by his deeds alone."

They said, "Not even you, O Messenger of Allah?"

The Prophet said, "Not even me unless Allah grants me His mercy. Know that the most beloved deed to Allah is that which is done regularly, even if it is small."
Sahih al-Bukhari 6467

If I understand the hadith above properly, it means even the Prophet (SAW) can't enter the final destination by his deeds alone. It gives hope to you and me. So if we are not judged by our deeds alone, then how are we evaluated?

In Islam, what matters is not the result but rather our sincere intentions and consistent actions and efforts. In other words, you do your best and Allah does the rest. You know and Allah (SWT) knows what that best is.

Journey vs. Destination

So what is the best way to live? Shall we just focus on the Destination? Or shall we just focus on Journey - how we live here? In other words: Deen or Dunya? This is a delusion that leads us to analysis paralysis. It is a trick by Satan, the outcasted one, to put us in a never-ending debate.

Here are some undeniable facts we all agree on: We are here only for a while until death catches upon us. We don't know when. As Muslims, we believe we are on our way to Our Creator. We live only once, and not in the sense that we can do whatever we want because we know we will be held to account. So, how can we live this life to the fullest that will be best here and hereafter?

What is required from us to succeed?

1. Sincere Intention (*ikhlas* and *niyyah* for His sake)
2. Consistent Action

Remember: we should not be bound to the outcome. Because we have to remember Who is in control.

We as Muslims have to remember that Allah (SWT) is in charge and every step we take and every move we make is recorded. They will never go to waste.

So whoever does an atom's weight of good will see it.
Quran, 99:7

We have to trust in Allah (SWT) that He will deliver His promise either in this world or the next, as long as our intentions are sincere and we sincerely do our best.

In the end, it is about our intention and attitude. We can decide to be bitter or better. We can be either Human Seeings or Human Beings. We can stay where we are and barely survive, or we can do our best to thrive. We can ask Allah (SWT) to help us to live our lives in the best way so we can prepare this life as our gift in the book of our life story, inshaAllah.

Blue Pill or Red Pill

I now present you with two options. In the movie "The Matrix," Morpheus presents Neo with two pills: blue and red. If he takes the blue pill, he will wake up in the world he used to know as if nothing happened. Or if he takes the red pill, Morpheus promises him to show another reality.

In a similar way, there are two ways to read this book:

1. You can read this book for your entertainment. You are welcome. You may find some personal stories you can share with others later.
2. You can also read this book with the intention to discover your purpose, your why, your passion, and your superpower so that you can create the story of your journey to Him that will allow you to serve in the best way. In doing so, you will not only find prosperity, but you will also enter a state of flow and a different reality that you don't have to escape any longer, inshaAllah.

One of my intentions in writing the book is not only to share my story and journey with you but to also help you discover your story for your life storybook to show on the day of judgment.

Imagine that we are holding our life story books in our right hands with joy on that Day. Is it not something worth living for?

If so, take this book as something not only you read, but also something you take action on.

I've provided your first action steps below. The first one is to do everything with a sincere intention, followed by consistent action..

"..Allah does not change a people until they change what is in themselves"
Quran, 13:11

Daily Du'a

Let's start our journey with a prayer to The Responding One (Al Mujeeb). Please, add these du'as to your daily prayers. If necessary, rephrase them as they sound natural to you but please keep their meanings intact:

I bear witness that there is nothing and no one worthy of worship/service to place in the center of my life except Allah, and I bear witness that Muhammad (SAW) is his servant and messenger.

O, Allah! I ask you to help me to get to know him and his life so I can follow his example in the best possible way.

O, Allah! Give us the best in this world and the next and save us from the fire.

O, Allah! Please, open my heart, open my mind, and guide me so I will discover for what reason You created me, so I will discover what special gifts and superpowers You have granted me, so I will use these gifts to serve You and You alone.

O, Allah! You have given me the best gift—the gift of life—witnessing all around and getting to know you and eventually loving you. While my good deeds will never be enough to enter your garden, I will ask for your mercy since you are The Most Merciful.

O, Allah! Guide me so that I live my life as You want me to live, so every step I take, and every move I make will be counted as my *ibadah*/service/worship to You. Make my whole life my gift to you to bring on the Last Day.

O, Allah! Help me on my journey to You, because You are The Best Helper. You are the Most Caring. You are the Most Kind. You are the Most Loving. You are the Most Generous. You are the Best Giver of Gifts.

Daily Prayers

Ideally, you should make these du'as after each of your five daily prayers. What if you don't pray yet? I'm not here to judge you. I have been on the other side as well. There were times I didn't pray too, because I didn't really understand. I thought if Allah was not in need of anyone or anything, why did He need my prayers? Actually, He didn't need my prayers. It was I who needed these daily prayers.

There are endless benefits of daily prayers. I will not count them all here. You can read about them on your own.

Which of the two choices did you choose? If you are just reading this book, then keep reading. Hopefully, you will gain some benefit.

On the other hand, if you are reading this book to implement these seven steps in order to change your life for the better, then starting on your daily prayers is a must. Treat the daily prayers as checkpoints. When we drive to a new location, we use GPS / Google Maps in our cars. One of the ways we make sure we reach our destination is to keep checking if we are following the map.

It is the same way on our spiritual life journeys. If you took Option 2, then you decided to implement these 7 steps. The first one is to make a sincere intention to submit our life in full to serve Allah and Allah alone. Even without knowing the full details yet, you should be proud that you took the first step.

This is why we are asking those things in our du'as. We will keep asking them every day. We may extend some of the du'as, but we will keep asking.

The five daily prayers will be our checkpoints throughout the day, and they only take a few minutes. If you don't pray at all, start praying once a day. Then twice a day. Until you start praying five times a day. The new way of life requires a new way of taking action. We will get there slowly.

If you are not already praying five times a day, then include this dua as well in your daily prayers:

O Allah! Thank You for guiding me to remember You every day. Please, keep me consistent in my daily prayers. Help me increase my daily prayers so I will pray at least five times a day as every Muslim should do.

Remember, your purpose in life is to serve/worship Allah **not part-time** but to willingly **submit to serve Him full-time** to fulfill your potential. You can do that if you live your life in a fully awake state (*fitrah*) where you are the Main Hero in your own story/life movie. Your story is that against all the odds through hardships in your life, you are on your way to Him, and to Him is your final return. As long as you are sincere in your intention and you walk toward Him, you will find Him running toward you.

What does it all mean? Spend some time thinking, contemplating, and reflecting (*tafakkur*) and doing the same in a way that encompasses your mind, heart, and soul (*tadabbur*). It is possible your mind may come up with hundreds of questions: "How do I do that? What do I do next?" Everything has its own timing. We will discuss those questions soon. For now, focus here and now. Allah (SWT) invited you to read this book. Now. You are here. This is what matters the most. Bismillah.

Action Steps for Step 1 (Purpose)

1. Ask Allah (SWT) to keep your intentions sincere and your actions consistent toward Him.

2. As Muslims we believe, everything is from Allah (SWT). If so, why did He invite you to read this book? Why now?

3. Write down how it looks like for you to serve Allah full-time, not part-time. Then ask Allah (SWT) to make it happen.

4. Ask Allah (SWT) to help you discover your purpose and live your life to the fullest potential as a main character in your life story so you are among the best of creation.

5. Strive to pray your five daily prayers, even if you start with one daily prayer at the start.

That's it for this chapter. I will see you inshallah in the next chapter where we will discuss your passion and superpower.

STEP 2 ~ PASSION

"You've got to find what you love. The only way to do great work is to love what you do. If you haven't found it yet, keep looking. Don't settle. As with all matters of the heart, you'll know when you find it."
—Steve Jobs, Co-founder of Apple Inc.

Do you like your life movie? Are you the main hero? Do you love what you do? Do you do what you love so it doesn't feel like work or a job? Are you great at what you do so you feel confident and others look up to you? What about helping others? Does your work create so much impact in others' lives that it is so fulfilling? Do you get paid well by doing what you love?

Flow is being completely involved in an activity for its own sake. The ego falls away. Time flies. Every action, movement, and thought follows inevitably from the previous one...
—Mihaly Csikszentmihalyi

Today, I can truly say that I love what I do. Alhamdulillah, I am good at what I do and I am getting better every day. My team and I serve millions of Muslims by helping Muslim Entrepreneurs and Professionals. We get paid well, alhamdulillah.

However, it was not always like this. If you asked me these questions 20 years ago, I would reply to you not to waste my time.

The Question I Hated The Most

You see, years ago I was in a different state: survival mode. Have you been there before? Are you there now?

This may sound familiar: I did everything I could legally do in order to earn money. Growing up in poverty in a single-parent household had a long-lasting impact.

As a child, the question I hated the most was: "What is your favorite color?" It is not that I didn't understand the question. I did. Let's say you have a blue pen, red pen, and green pen. With those three pens in front of you, the questions "What is your favorite color? Which one do you like better?" are easy.

My problem was: I didn't have a pen at all. Not a blue one, a red one, or a green one. So when you presented a pen to me, it didn't matter what color it was. I would take any pen with any color.

The moral of the story is that you can't think about passion when you are in survival mode. It is a luxury.

Fast forward to today, and I know my favorite color. I know even the favorite colors of my kids. What changed? Now I can afford to buy things for myself and my family. They have options. They have a choice.

Money-Driven Only

Most people live just in the pursuit of money. In my first 10 years abroad in Denmark, I got a house, a car, and a well-paid job, alhamdulillah. But as I said earlier, something was missing.

We need money only to a certain point, but then it has a lesser and lesser effect on the quality of our lives. If you are reading this, you are one of two states: either you have been through what I am describing and you know what I am talking about, or you are still on your way and you may think, "No way. If I only had money, I could get anything in life!"

But if money isn't everything, what is?

Passion-Driven Only

Then you see some people, who talk only about passion, passion, and passion. I love this and I love that. Unfortunately, I see that most of them are also broke, financially. What comes to my mind are countless artists, singers, and people who mainly deal with self-expression and art.

These people think only about their passion and themselves. They may miss the part about how their work will serve others (remember, Step 1 is Purpose!) and how they can turn it into something valuable that others will support. Without these missing parts, these people will not make it.

But if passion isn't everything, what is?

Ikigai

If money or passion is not enough, what is? I am glad you asked. There is a better and balanced middle path. In the first section, we talked about finding your purpose.

When we as Muslims as well as human beings seek our purpose in life, we eventually discover that our purpose is to serve God by serving His creation. So how do we serve? Once you understand that you are here to serve *humanity* (God doesn't need our service), your passion becomes easier to uncover.

So the question is, how do we *best* serve Him? This is a question I've been asking myself for the last 10 years. I've found the best example to illustrate this point and have found it in the Japanese term *ikigai*.

Ikigai: (生き甲斐, literally. 'a reason for being') is a Japanese concept referring to something that gives a person a sense of purpose, a reason for living. It encompasses four primary elements:

1.   what you love (your unique passion - your superpower),
2.   what the world needs (your mission - how you serve Allah SWT by serving others),
3.   what you are good at (your work - your profession), and
4.   how you can make a living by doing what you love.

Ikigai

A JAPANESE CONCEPT MEANING "A REASON FOR BEING"

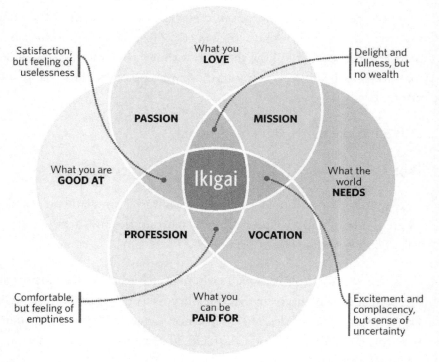

How do you find your Ikigai? It requires some thinking and some alone time. Go for a walk in nature. You can also go to a room where you are alone. Take some paper and a pen, but no device. Make a du'a: "Oh, Allah! Open my heart and my mind so that I will discover the gifts You have given me so I can serve You by serving Your creation in the best way." Then ask these questions.

What Do I Love?

What would you do for hours that are so fulfilling to you, even if no one paid you? What are the things that when you do them, you lose track of time? Make a list of as many of those things as possible and write them down one by one. Treat it as a brainstorming session. Keep writing. You need at least 3 to 5 things you love. If you have 10, even better.

What Does the World Need?

How does this thing you love connect with your purpose of serving God, by serving His creation? Ask this for each thing you love that you listed in the question above.

The next element of ikigai is what the world needs, your mission. As we discussed in Step 1 Purpose, this is the most important thing. Aligning with your purpose will not only give meaning to your journey but also gives you a reality check that what you love to do can actually benefit others, not just yourself. This is extremely important because helping others leaves our souls feeling satisfied, and draws us nearer to God.

For example, you may love lying on the beach. You may love it and even be good at it, but who benefits from you lying on the beach besides yourself? The key here is to hone in on the things that help you and benefit others at the same time. The intersection of what you love and what benefits the world is what we are trying to uncover. Spend some time pondering what the world currently needs. What are some major and minor social issues? Do you see any overlap with areas that interest you?

What am I Good at?

Next, let's examine another element of ikigai–what you are good at. You may be good at math, drawing, or computer programming. If you're not sure what you're good at, consider what others compliment you on. What have colleagues or previous superiors told you that you do well? Did you receive formal recognition for work performed or an award or acknowledgment? Begin writing a list of what you are good at, including personal accomplishments for which you have been recognized. This exercise aims to get to know yourself better before diving head-first into your business.

Are you good at any of the things you love to do?

How Do I Get Paid?

You now want to list things that you love doing that you can get paid for. This can be uncovered by detailing tasks you have done in the past for income. Also, add jobs to the lists that you would like to be compensated for. When your "what the world needs" and your "what I can be paid for" lists align, all that's left to do is to learn the business side, and all other elements will quickly fall into place. There are many ways to make money from what you love and what you are good at. Ideally, you want to couple those passions with a solution that solves a problem for someone. When all the pieces come together, you'll realize that you can get paid for doing what you enjoy *while* helping people.

Connecting the Dots

Once you check all the boxes on the four elements of *ikigai*, you come away with work that is both meaningful and worthy of doing. Passion alone is not enough, because if you cannot figure out how to make money from your passion, you won't be able to transition it from a hobby to work that is sustainable financially. We aim to find something for you that's worth making a living from—to find purposeful work that becomes the main thread of your life.

Frequently people find that when they apply themselves to work that they genuinely care about, they naturally elevate to being among the best in their field. When you do things you love and that the world needs, it can become your mission. When you combine your passion with your mission, you get an irreverent sense of satisfaction from your work.

But I don't want you to settle for just finding your passion, going after a significant mission, or achieving a certain level of education. My advice would be to strive for excellence that is exhibited when all of these essential elements meet. I want to believe that you can have it all and go after your heart's desire, especially when it comes to the work that you focus on in your life.

Delight, but No Wealth

Look at the *ikigai* diagram again. Maybe you find something you love, are good at, and that the world needs, but you cannot get paid for it. At the top of the diagram, you see you can be delighted and full but have no wealth. Consequently, if no wealth is involved, your work may still be doable but present challenges. Without financial means, you may not be able to offer your family a good life; of course, we all want a good life with our families that allow us to provide them with a good education, food, shelter, etc. So while attaining wealth is not the sole focus, we also don't want to be in a position where we don't have sufficient means.

Feeling of No Purpose

Let's look at another example. Say you find work you love, are good at, and can even be compensated for. However, if your work consists of things the world doesn't need, you may feel some sort of complacency.

You can feel satisfaction from doing constructive work and still feel you need to improve if you're solving a problem. A good example of this is found in some YouTube personalities, who make videos with no particular point and may feel useless because they're not solving a real problem.

Feeling Empty

Alternatively, you might be in a position of doing what you're good at, being paid for it, and the world needs it, yet you may not love it—your passion lies elsewhere. It's comfortable, but the feeling that something is missing causes you to continue to ponder other career paths.

Feeling Uncertain

Lastly, you might love your work, the world needs it, and you're being paid for it, but you may feel you're not good (or not good enough) at it. Perhaps you're struggling in your work, and your skills are not where you want them to be. Not feeling like your work is good enough can lead to uncertainty because certainty and confidence come from being good at what you do.

As you seek to gain a better understanding of this multi-layered philosophy, I'd ask you to focus on 'what you love' *first*. This is because when you find what you love, your passion lies there, and with time and effort, you can also become skilled at your optimum passion.

From Stutterer to Speaking World Champion

I recently interviewed Mohammed Qahtani - the 2015 Public Speaking World Champion. On his first day of school, his teacher scolded him for stuttering and told him that he would never amount to anything.

Mohammed believed in what his teacher said. For the next few years, he didn't speak at all in class, all the way until high school. Then a friend suggested that Mohammed could speak, but told him that he needed to challenge himself by making the school's morning announcements.

The first time Mohammed made the announcements, he stuttered. Everyone laughed. He was ashamed and went back to his friend in defeat. But his friend encouraged him to keep trying and gave him hope that eventually, he would improve.

Mohammed persevered. He kept making the school announcements every morning. He began to stutter less and less. Fewer and fewer people laughed. He also joined a Toastmasters Public Speaking club. He knew it would take years to master public speaking, but he kept at it. In 2015, he became a World Champion of Public Speaking.

Mohammed's story is incredible. He faced his most avoided fear–speaking–and kept at it until he mastered it. Now public speaking is his passion and purpose. He is great at it and he gets paid all around the world. I encourage you to watch his award-winning speech here: www.deenpreneurs.net/champion

Life Mastery

Canadian journalist and New York Times bestselling author Malcolm Gladwell has popularized a notion called the 10,000 rule. The rule states that it takes about 10,000 hours of intensive practice to achieve mastery of complex skills and materials. That translates to ten years of study.

Would you spend ten years studying something you weren't passionate about? Of course not!

Ottoman Schools Motto

In Ottoman Schools, every child was evaluated due to his/her talents and every child had different courses. The Motto of the schools was written on the walls:

"Here No Fish will be forced to Fly and No Bird will be forced to Swim"

My Ikigai

We learn by example and by doing, not just by theory. That's why I want to share with you some examples of how I myself have implemented the *ikigai* approach into my own life. It has allowed me to help others in the form of helping Muslim entrepreneurs. In doing so, I discovered by experience that one of the best things in life is to do meaningful work that helps others. It brings true satisfaction to the soul.

Ten years ago, when I decided to start my business, it was because I wasn't feeling fulfilled. I was at a point where I was paid well, good at my job, and solving a problem; I was a part of the team. I worked at a company called Vestas, which made wind turbines. Yet still, I thought, this is not something I *love* doing. That love is what I was lacking, and I just felt a sense of emptiness.

I was also soul-searching during this time; I wanted to find my purpose and do something impactful, but I just didn't know what it was. That was around the time I came across the concept of *ikigai*, so I started creating my own list of things I loved to do. Here was the list of things I loved at that time: design, startups, entrepreneurship, Islam, learning, and serving the Ummah.

This list would expand and change at a later point in my life, which is normal. After I made the list, I didn't know what to do or how it would play a role in the next phase of my life.

What I did know is that I wanted to follow my purpose and my passion somehow and someway. So I made a du'a to Allah (SWT): "O, Allah! Help me to find a way so whatever I do will be a full-time service for You in this world and the next."

The answer to that prayer began to unfold in my own life story. It started through an old friend of mine named Jamaliddin. Together, we started the world's first social network for Muslims called Ummaland. You can read the full story later in the book. While it was not a success financially, it was the starting point for Halal.Ad and many more ventures to come. One of those ventures is Quran Era.

Quran Era

This adventure started through yet another old friend of mine named Nadir, who I have had the privilege of getting to know very well while we both studied in Denmark. He is originally from Uzbekistan like me. He's known for being very kind, and also passionate about teaching the Quran. In fact, I have even taken Quran lessons from him.

He moved from Denmark to Australia and settled there with his family. He and I kept in touch, as he studied and taught Down Under and I also studied and worked in Denmark.

He followed the work I was doing with different startups and companies, and I followed his work as well. And at one point, he reached out to me, saying he wanted to create something to help teach the Quran to children. "That's great," I told him, "Just go do it. You don't need my help because you are an excellent Quran teacher."

He replied, "No—I want to do something special here, but I don't know exactly what that is." That prompted us to have a deeper conversation.

I'm telling you his story because it is an excellent example of what we've been covering. I knew he was passionate about teaching the

Quran, but he hadn't outlined the other principles of *ikigai* that would create a foundation for what he was trying to achieve. He needed to take time to specify the things he was good at, what particular problem he could solve, and how he would be paid for his concept.

He was clearly passionate about teaching the Quran to children. But he needed to figure out the other pieces to the puzzle. For six months to a year, we had ongoing conversations about his goal, where we would ping-pong ideas back and forth between each other. He wanted to do something different than what was already being offered, but couldn't quite figure it out.

Eventually, I said to him, "Look, if you're just doing a basic Quran academy, I don't think that's going to be enough. It's been done, repeatedly. What you really need is something unique and meaningful to the Ummah, something that no one else is doing."

These conversations and ideas were the early stages of a startup company that Nadir and I co-founded, now known as Quran Era, an online Quran reading app that teaches how to read the Quran the most fun way via games, video stories, songs, and many other activities.

When it came to purpose, Nadir and I were aligned. As Prophet (SAW) said: "The best among you are those who learn and teach the Quran." Our purpose was to serve Allah SWT by teaching Muslim children to get introduced to His Book in the most fun way, while also teaching them how to read the Quran in the best way.

Nadir and I also had aligned passions. He had been learning and teaching the Quran for years.

Yet, these two elements—passion and purpose—were still not enough on their own to get us to what is now a world-class product that thousands of Muslim children love, and that thousands of Muslim parents pay to access.

Chapter Three explains more about the next step we needed to take. For now, however, let's review what we learned in this chapter through the next set of action steps.

Action Steps for Step 2 (Passion)

1. Ask Allah to guide you and help you to discover your purpose and passion, so you can best serve Him.

2. Write down your reflections on the four *ikigai* elements:

   - What you love (things that put you in a flow state)
   - What the world needs (your mission)
   - What you are good at (your skills, talents)
   - What you can earn an income from (get paid)

Be sure to do each action step carefully, especially step two. Don't rush through this step; you may want to ask a spouse or close friend, or family member to help you with some options here if they do not come to you easily. Try to aim for a minimum of three items for each element, but more items are preferred. This will give you plenty of ideas to work with as we expound upon them later.

STEP 3 ~ PRODUCT

How do you turn your purpose and passion into a product that solves a problem, and that others are willing to pay for it? Is it even possible?

The answer is yes! In this chapter, I will continue to share a personal example of how we have done exactly that when it comes to our company Quran Era, and how we have used this experience to help many Muslim entrepreneurs and professionals on their journeys as well.

To recap, Step 1 involved finding your purpose in terms of your personal fulfillment and your role in the world. In Step 2, you explored your passions and identified your strengths.

Now, in Step 3, we will focus on creating a solution. You can think of this solution as a product. We will "produce" a specific solution for a specific problem of specific people, and one that is in line with our purpose and fueled by our passion.

The "solution" can be a service, a physical product, or anything else. This step aims to bring together all that you've learned about intention (*niyyah*), purpose (serving Allah), passions, and strengths and use them

71

to find a solution to a real problem.

Which Path is Right for You?

Before we go further, I would like to take a pause here and ask you a question: Are you a Muslim entrepreneur or a Muslim professional?

Let me rephrase. Are you willing to turn your purpose and passion into a product or service, one that is a specific solution to a specific problem or a specific group of people? Are you then willing to market, then sell it, then deliver your promise so you can get paid?

If your answers are yes, you are part of a specific group of Muslim entrepreneurs that I like to call Deenpreneurs. While the journey of Deenpreneuar is not easy, it is doable and fulfilling. If this is you, read the book as it is and implement the actions one step at a time. Create your own journey. Be your own boss.

Being a Deenpreneur comes with responsibility as well, not only with privileges. For Deenpreneurs, problems are opportunities. They present a chance to listen, learn, and find a solution. Not everyone is interested in solving problems and creating a product or service, and that's okay.

Maybe you are not that type of person, and maybe the entrepreneurial approach seems like too much for you. That's ok as well–only 5 to 10% of the population are entrepreneurs. Some Muslim brothers and sisters may prefer to follow a traditional career path and work for a company rather than start their own, for a variety of reasons. If that's you, you're more accurately described as a Muslim professional.

Both approaches have value. Some people are driven to become entrepreneurs, while the rest are better suited to helping others, such as working within a company. Maybe you are a Muslim professional with a specific skill set who wants to join a team who are aligned with your purpose and passion. In that case, read the book from the perspective of understanding how companies and business work in general. This will help you add more value. And the more value you add, the more valuable you are. This will pave the way for you to get a better position and better opportunities in your company. If your company is not aligned with your purpose and passion, it is time to move on.

3 Advice for Deenpreneurs

I asked a friend Chris Blauvelt - a co-founder and CEO of Launch Good (www.launchgood.com) to share some advice for Muslim entrepreneurs. Here is what he shared.

1. Learn to be a great follower and supporter before becoming a leader;
2. Spend your 20s learning as much as you can, then bring it together as you approach your 30s;
3. Find a great cofounder (or 2) you can really trust.

Why, Will, Way

You may know the popular saying. "Where there's a will, there's a way."

That is definitely true. However, one of the toughest parts of that equation that we often dismiss is: How do you find that will?

It seems that they omitted the first part! So I came up with the first part. I hope you will find it useful ●:

> *Where there's a why, there is a will.*
> *Where there's a will, there is a way.*
> —*Maruf Yusuf*

All jokes aside, we all know that life is not all butterflies and rainbows. It is tough. No one gets out alive. What we believe reflects in our actions. Our actions will then reflect in our reality.

Most business books start by stating that the only purpose of business is making money. Some books don't even state that, because they start from the assumption that it is true. Then we Muslims along with everybody read these books. We will start implementing the same mindset in our lives.

Sadly, what happens next is that our actions, as Muslims, don't end up matching our beliefs. What I mean is that we may say "la ilaha illa Allah," but we don't really understand or live out the true meaning.

Money becomes a god. This is a serious pitfall for Muslim entrepreneurs as well as Muslim professionals.

On the other hand, as Muslim professionals, we may go to universities because our parents chose those career paths for us: lawyers, engineers, or whatever makes more money. Then we climb the corporate ladder to be famous, to gain power, to be popular, and to get paid more, all while forgetting why we do what we do. Where is Allah (SWT) in that equation?

It comes as no surprise that we are stuck in jobs we hate or companies we don't enjoy working for.

This is why we started with Purpose—so you know why you do what you do. Then we looked inwards to discover your Passion—so you enjoy what you do. Because it is going to be a long journey. It will not be easy. But we will come through together, inshaAllah.

Something's Gotta Give

Here is an example from my daily life. Let's take the process of writing this book. You may be reading this book and thinking, "I don't see any issues." However, you may not know that I am not fond of writing, to put it mildly. I have been trying to write this book for years but kept postponing it.

I kept speaking with Muslim entrepreneurs and professionals every week. Most of them were not yet ready for our marketing agency to help, so I would have to send them away. I really want to have somewhere else to send them, a place where they could be guided to follow a series of steps that would help them to prepare and come back when they were ready. It bothered me that I didn't have the book available.

The book was begging me to write it, but when I recently turned 40 the call became stronger. As a 40-year-old, I knew that from now on, I was going to be living the last part of my life on Earth. I said to myself, "If I don't start this book now, when will I?" The unfortunate and sudden death of Sh. Muhammad Alshareef - one of my mentors was the last straw that broke the camel's back.

I needed to make writing the book a habit. One of the things I learned from my habits course is that there is more than one way of creating habits. Maybe I dislike writing–ok. But what if there is another way of recording my thoughts? I needed to think outside the box.

I walk every day. So I started dictating my thoughts. Then, I sent those recordings to a service where they transcribed them. Part of the book is written like that. I also experimented with going to a meeting with a person and talking about my ideas, while recording. Later I shared that video, and the person would transcribe and edit it as well.

After all of this, I went through the content and edited as much as I could. I then shared the book with a couple of other editors who helped clean up the styling and develop the ideas.

What kept me going during this process was my *why*–remembering why I do what I do. Why am I writing this book? Who am I writing this book for and how this will serve my Muslim brothers and sisters as my service to Allah SWT?

My why led to my will, which led to my way!

I even used the same approaches that I am sharing with you to write this book. Even though I knew there was a need for this information, I had to verify the need. So I reached out to my LinkedIn network and asked. People responded, and I valued their input. Then I asked for their help in choosing a title. They responded again. Then I asked for input in choosing the book cover. They responded once more.

We marketed this book based on a promise to you, the reader. Now the book is in your hands. Based on the knowledge in this book and how committed you are, we will see how well we deliver the promise, inshaAllah.

Your journey will be different from mine, but they will be similar in many ways as well, inshaAllah. Knowing and believing in your Purpose—your *why*—will help you get through. Knowing and following your Passion will make this journey as pleasant as possible, inshaAllah.

Now that I have explained the reality of the journey without rose-colored glasses on, I hope you are mentally, emotionally, and more importantly spiritually ready to continue it with me.

It may not be easy, but it is worth it.

Bismillah.

The Million Dollar Question

In the middle of difficulty lies opportunity.
—Albert Einstein

What specific problem can you solve (your purpose) better than anyone (your *ikigai*) for specific people (your market) so good that they are willing to pay for it?

If you can answer this question, you are much closer than anyone to making your business a success, inshaAllah. That's because every successful business solves a problem for some people who are willing to pay for it. This is called **value creation**. You may know hundreds or maybe even thousands of businesses or companies, but they all fall into one or more of the 12 standard forms of value.

The concept of the 12 standard forms of value is described in the book "The Personal MBA" by Josh Kaufman. It is a must-read if you haven't read it yet. Once you know these 12 forms of value, you will not only recognize what value the businesses around you offer, but you also will be in a better position to come up with a clear concept of what value your company offers.

12 Standard Forms of Value

To provide value to another person, it must take on a form that they are willing to pay for. Economic Value usually takes one of the following *12 Standard Forms of Value*:

#	Value	Description	Example
1	**Product**	Create a single tangible item or entity, then sell and deliver it for more than what it cost to make.	A book.
2	**Service**	Provide help or assistance then charge a fee for the benefits rendered	A barber.
3	**Shared Resource**	Create a durable asset that can be used by many people, then charge for access.	Car rental.
4	**Subscription**	Offer a benefit on an ongoing basis and charge a recurring fee.	Quran Era, Netflix, etc.
5	**Resale**	Acquire an asset from a wholesaler, then sell that asset to a retail buyer at a higher price.	Retail shop.
6	**Lease**	Acquire an asset, then allow another	Car lease.

		person to use that asset for a pre-defined amount of time in exchange for a fee.	
7	**Agency**	Market and sell an asset or service you don't own on behalf of a third party, then collect a percentage of the transaction price as a fee.	Real estate agent.
8	**Audience Aggregation**	Get the attention of a group of people with certain characteristics, then sell and access in the form of advertising to another business looking to reach those audiences.	Facebook, Instagram, LinkedIn, Tiktok, etc.
9	**Loan***	Lend a certain amount of money, then collect payments over a pre-defined period of time equal to the original loan plus a pre-defined interest rate.* *Please note that usual interest rates are not allowed in Islam.	Islamic banks that offer interest-free loans.
10	**Option**	Offer the ability to take a pre-defined action for a fixed period of time in exchange for a fee.	A movie ticket.
11	**Insurance**	Take on the risk of some specific bad thing happening to the policyholder in exchange for a pre-defined series of payments, then pay out claims only when the bad thing actually happens.	Car insurance.
12	**Capital**	Purchase an ownership stake in a business, then collect a corresponding portion of the profit as a one-time payout or ongoing dividend.	Investing in a company or stock.

The Importance of Creating Value

Any company you know fits into one or more of these 12 categories.

Now that you know the 12 forms of creating value, how can you create more value as a Deenpreneur or Muslim Professional which can lead to better jobs, higher salaries, and more opportunities?

To do this, it's essential to look inward and identify the problems that interest you and that you're good at solving.

Ask yourself:

- What problems are out there that I find interesting?
- What am I great at that puts me/my product/my company/my service in a position to solve the problem better than anybody else?

By putting yourself, your product, or your service in a position to solve the problem better than anyone else, you'll be able to stand out.

It reminds me of the story of Joe Bradford. I interviewed Brother Joe for our podcast where he shared his story of how he became an Islamic Finance Advisor. He has been in this sector for the last 15 years at least, and he is one of the go-to advisors.

How did he get started? He noticed that elders in his masjid called Islamic scholars overseas to get advice about Islamic finance questions in the USA. He watched the whole process and realized how ineffective it was. That was the starting point for him, and he wanted to do something about it. So he did.

I also asked Sister Shelina Janmohamed - VP of Islamic Marketing at Ogilvy and the author of "Generation M: Young Muslims Changing The World" about creating. Here is what she shared:

"The most inspiring thing when you're on your journey to create something new is also the most daunting: finding the gap. You see the gap and you think 'how has nobody done this before?' 'how can there be a gap?' Some people won't believe that there's a gap. Sometimes you won't even believe yourself. Some people won't recognize the need – they'll say there isn't a requirement.

That's the daunting part – you need to scope it and have the strong feeling to bring it to life. But that gap is also the most exciting thing – you can make a difference. And sometimes the most surprising part is how simple the question is that you need to ask. How obvious it is. And if you see a gap, be the solution to your own problem. Because if you don't solve it, who will?"

What is a burning question you want to answer? What keeps you awake at night?

Mindful and Purpose-Driven Entrepreneurship

Before starting this journey, it's important to remember that this book is not just for entrepreneurs but specifically for Muslim entrepreneurs. To ensure that what we create aligns with our purpose, we must be mindful and seek guidance from Allah (SWT).

Our intention (*niyyah*) should always guide us in serving others in the best possible way. We ask Allah for His help and inspiration in finding the best solution to a problem. We start with a sincere intention and then consider the four stages of the process.

Generating Ideas

How do you come up with an idea for your next big thing? It could come to you anywhere, at any time.

Consider the story of Junaid Wahedna, a good friend and the CEO of Wahed Invest. One day Junaid took a taxi cab in New York City and on his way, he talked to the driver. It turns out that the driver was also a Muslim. They chatted a bit. Then the driver complained about the lack of halal investment options. The driver explained that he opted to keep all of his money in cash since he didn't want to deal with banks that deal in interest.

For many of us, that conversation would be nothing special. For Junaid, who already had a keen sense of his own purpose and passion, it was the catalyst for his idea to launch Wahed Invest. As of March 2023, Wahed Invest serves over 300,000 Muslim investors and is valued at around $500 million, according to Crunchbase.

One lesson to take away from this story is this: listen to your customers first. Another is to keep an open mind to opportunities that might present themselves in unexpected ways.

Examples like these don't tell us exactly what to do, but they offer us wise guidance. Similarly, while this book doesn't spell out your exact pathway to success, it does provide you with tried and true questions that you can ask yourself in order to open that path.

Painkiller vs. Vitamin

When you're thinking of a new product or service idea, you can think of it in terms of a painkiller or a vitamin.

A painkiller in this context would be something that solves a specific problem or pain point that people have. Just like how a painkiller helps relieve a headache, a painkiller product or service addresses a problem that people are experiencing and provides a solution. It makes their lives easier or better by solving a particular issue they are facing.

For example, if people have trouble finding parking spaces in a crowded city, you could create an app that helps them locate available parking spots easily. Your product or service becomes like a painkiller by directly addressing and solving their problem.

On the other hand, a vitamin in this context would be something that adds value to people's lives, even if they don't have a specific problem. Just like how vitamins provide extra nutrients to keep our bodies healthy, a vitamin product or service enhances people's lives in a positive way. It may not solve a pressing problem, but it brings enjoyment, convenience, or additional benefits to their daily routine.

For example, creating a social networking app where people can connect with friends and share their interests is like a vitamin because it adds fun and social interaction to their lives.

So, as an entrepreneur, you can think about whether your product or service idea is like a painkiller, addressing a specific problem and providing a solution, or if it's more like a vitamin, adding value and enhancing people's lives even if they don't have a pressing problem.

Both approaches have their own merits and can be successful, depending on the needs and desires of your target customers.

Remember, as an entrepreneur, it's important to understand your customers' needs and find ways to create products or services that either solve their problems or bring value to their lives. By doing so, you can create something that people truly want and make a positive impact on the world.

If this is your first time, my suggestion is to start with a painkiller product. It will be easier to market and sell it. Your painkiller should work so well that people are willing to give you their hard-earned cash to relieve their headache. The larger the headache market, the better it is. On your next product, you can experiment with a vitamin.

Four Stages of the Product Development Process

The journey of a product or service has four stages. These are also sometimes called the "4 Stages to Scale":

1. Ideation
2. MVP (Minimum Viable Product)
3. PMF (Product Market Fit)
4. Growth

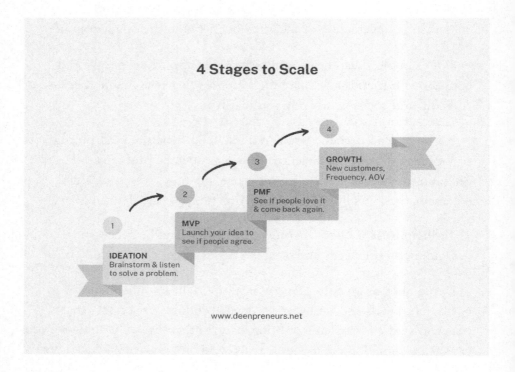

Stage 1: Ideation

In this stage, you are brainstorming. Based on your purpose and passion, you are trying to come up with a solution for specific people that are willing to pay for it. Purpose helps you keep moving. Passion makes your journey more enjoyable, inshaAllah. If you build something so helpful that people are willing to pay, use it, and even refer to their family and friends, it means you got the main core elements of your business right.

This is much easier said than done. Before you go too far considering an idea, there are two more things that I strongly advise you to keep in mind: **sharing your ideas** and **building your team**.

Here's why:

One of the most common questions I get asked is: "Shall I tell my idea to others? What if they steal my idea?" Sooner or later, you need to launch your idea and test it. Sooner or later, people will see your "secret" idea. Unless you patent your idea, people will copy your idea sooner or later.

If your idea needs to be patented, definitely protect your intellectual property. But if sharing your idea with key individuals is the only way it will develop, that's critical too.

I say that because I've learned that success is not only about ideas. Firstly, the idea should be the right one for the market. The timing of the idea should be right as well. You then need a great team and funds to bring your idea into the world.

But the most challenging part is: You don't know if your idea is the right one or the timing until you launch and test it in the market! So, don't be afraid of sharing your ideas with other people.

When you share your ideas with people, you will notice that while some may be indifferent, others will encourage you. Some of them even want to go on this journey with you. This is especially true if you share your ideas well and why you are doing what you are doing. The world is filled with people who are seeking meaning and impact. When looking for teammates, look for those with whom you can work and who will also complement your skills and talents. If you are a designer, you will need a developer. If you are a developer, look for someone who is good in marketing or sales. Sometimes you need to look for teammates to get you through the stage you are in.

This theory is good. But how is it done in practice?

Let me continue the story of Quran Era, as another example of how this approach can play out. My co-founder, Nadir, identified teaching the Quran to children as his purpose and passion and serving Allah. However, even after having a clear sense of purpose and passion, there was still uncertainty about how to turn it into a product.

One of the initial ideas was to open an online Quran academy. Still, we quickly realized that this would be just one of many academies, and it would be difficult to differentiate our approach. Sometimes the most obvious first solutions aren't the best.

When refining your idea to create a product, it's crucial to return to your why and your goal. Our goal, like with any startup I work with, is to aim high and serve millions of people—in this case, we wanted to serve at least a million Muslim children in learning how to read the Quran in a fun way. To achieve this specific goal, we had to consider specific factors.

To create a successful product, it's important to offer something unique and easily replicable, which is often a digital solution. In the case of Quran Era, again, our goal was to create the most fun, creative, and enjoyable way for kids to learn to read the Quran.

If your product/service can impact millions and if you can prove that you found a great product market fit, your chance of getting a seed investment increases. This is what we call a startup.

On the other hand, if you are building a lifestyle business that will impact your local community and generate a good living for you and your family, it is also ok. You just need to know what you are building and for what reason.

So, what's your specific goal?

MVP - Minimum Viable Product

In the ideation stage, much of what we create is based on assumptions—assumptions about what the final product will be, and assumptions about how others will receive it. The keyword here is assumptions—and those assumptions need to be tested.

Everyone has a plan until they get punched in the mouth.
—Mike Tyson

One of the common mistakes many entrepreneurs make is to jump to the full version of the product. Please, don't! It will save you tons of money and time. You will thank me later. Instead, come up with a **minimum viable product (MVP)**.

Test the market and your assumptions with your MVP. If it still makes sense, then you can do the full development. But chances are, you will gain feedback that will help you tweak and improve your idea.

In the case of Quran Era, my co-founder Nadir came up with a minimum viable product (drawings with Arabic letter characters and stories) that combined teaching Arabic through storytelling. We felt strongly that this was a promising start because it was innovative and unique.

In fact, this thoughtful idea from Nadir is what drew me toward the idea of the Quran Era start-up. It was incredibly creative and unique, and I hadn't seen a product like it. I was excited about the potential of creating something different in the market. So, I joined him on his journey as a co-founder.

My co-founder also then tested the method by teaching it to his own son, and it was a success.

Even then, before launching anything, he continued to use the Quran Era method of teaching Arabic through storytelling via this minimum viable product in order to learn and improve our product.

How? He taught at one of the Islamic schools on Sundays. The kids really enjoyed it and could memorize the material. Even though they only had class once a week, they retained what they learned by making connections. This showed us we had a unique, and effective, way of teaching the kids the letters they were memorizing.

PMF - Product-Market Fit

After you launch your MVP to the market, it is a reality check. Watch and listen to how people interact with your product or service. You should track not only how many people buy, but how many of them come back and buy again.

Of course, it depends on your product. If it is a subscription, then you should track your retention rate month over month. If you are selling a product that people need every week, then your weekly total will be the main data you need to track. And so on.

The idea is to build a product so good that people buy it, use it, and come back again. They tell their friends and they become your ambassadors.

The key is to bring a product to the market that solves a problem in a unique way, so much so that it makes your competitor's product irrelevant. In this way, you actually create your own market. You can learn more about this in the book "Blue Ocean Strategy" by Renée Mauborgne and W. Chan Kim.

If you want to master one skill, then master this skill of how to bring a product or service to the market—a product or service that is so great that many people are willing to pay for it without much hesitation.

20% of businesses fail within the first year, and 50% fail within the first five years. The most common reason businesses fail is that there's no

market for their product or service (42%).
*Source: **Bureau of Labor Statistics** and **Guidant Financial***

The Quran Era Journey, Continued

When assessing whether the Quran Era product was a good fit for the market, we moved on to the next stage of the product cycle, which was product market fit. We wanted to know if the school-tested product would be successful on a larger scale.

To find out, we launched a campaign on LaunchGood and felt thrilled to see that hundreds of people bought it for their own kids. This told us they saw the product, liked it, and purchased it, giving us even more validation.

The success of our project gave us a sense of confidence and satisfaction that we were doing something great, alhamdulillah. We launched the project in the summer of 2020, during the COVID-19 pandemic, and within just a few months, we had hundreds of views and surpassed 1,000 members. This was a remarkable achievement for us and showed us we had a product-market fit.

However, every company has its own cycle and terms. In our case, for Quran Era, we offered trials to potential customers and found that the success rate was at least 80%. This means that out of 10 people given access, at least eight of them signed up within a week or two.

For us, a product-market fit of 80% was a good number. It meant that most people who tried our product loved it and activated their subscriptions. This proved to us that our product was a good fit for the market.

Growth

The next stage in the product cycle is called the growth cycle, which is crucial for Muslim entrepreneurs to understand. When developing a product or service, it's important to go through all the stages, including fundraising, and be prepared to scale.

With Quran Era, the digital platform is scalable. The number of users, whether it's a thousand or a million, doesn't affect our technology. It's cost-effective to provide access to more users. This is the advantage software companies have, as they can easily distribute their product once it's developed. Integrating technology into your idea, if applicable, is a great way to take advantage of the nearly unlimited scalability found in the digital world.

Just because Quran Era is successful doesn't mean that we've finished all the work. In fact, we currently have only completed 60% of the Quran Era content! There is still so much room for growth. But that didn't stop us from the initial launch. To finance this growth, we are reaching out to investors, which is covered in the prosperity and finance chapter.

I will also share more about the Growth Stage in the next chapter.

Determining Your Entrepreneurial Goals

It's important to consider the potential for growth when developing a product, especially if you decide that you want to create a large "unicorn" startup with a valuation of at least $1 billion.

To create something impactful, you need to have a clear goal in mind. Some people want to create a small, sustainable business, while others want to create a large-scale, unicorn startup.

Our goal at Quran Era is to reach at least 1 million kids worldwide with our digital platform. We believe that if you have something truly valuable, you share it with as many people as possible. And we believe that millions of kids need better ways to learn the Quran.

There are 2 billion Muslims worldwide, and half of them are

children! That means 1 billion Muslim kids, 80% of whom don't speak Arabic. As parents and educators, we want to teach kids how to read the Quran, and we found that the best way to do that is to teach kids in the way that they want to learn. Even if we can reach 1 out of every 1,000 children, we would still have reached a total of 1 million, inshaAllah!

We know that children love playing on devices; I see that with my kids all the time. So we combined that fact with the notion that they also love to play in general. We knew that if we could present our story-telling approach not on an education platform but as something kids love playing, we could teach them without making them feel like they're in class. We believe that is the best way to teach kids how to learn the Quran.

With our method, learning becomes akin to gamification; gaming plus activities creates a learning journey. When kids start our program, they go country by country, learning different concepts and playing while they learn, and importantly it *feels* like play.

Once we had all those critical elements in place, making money from the product was an easy next step. We came to the market with a unique solution—the most fun and engaging way to teach kids how to read the Quran independently. Even without a parent constantly being hands-on, we saw that giving kids the device was enough for many of them (depending on age) to go through the material and learn individually.

In terms of the economic structure of the product, we wanted to keep it simple. We offer monthly and yearly payment options. We have recently exceeded 10,000 subscribers, but our goal is eventually to reach at least 1 million subscribers. We have started working with teachers, alhamdulillah, who are using the app in their classrooms, and we are also working with Islamic schools to roll out the app for large educational use. Alhamdulillah, we've been on this journey for two years, and I am pleased with the progress that has been made and what's next for this journey.

Perfect Example

Quran Era is a perfect example of what's possible for you and your business once you've done the foundational work to set your business up for success. When you apply the framework I've outlined here, it gives you a clear path to success.

My friend and my co-founder of Quran Era moved from Australia back to Uzbekistan. We now have a small team of seven or eight people there who are core members, and a few other part-time team members, but we are still growing.

This project is one of our *ikigais*, giving those involved a sense of purpose. Every time we hear from parents how excited their kids are after using the app, it just gives us such a sense of satisfaction and gratitude that we get to do what we do. It affirms to me, as someone who genuinely wants to help Muslim entrepreneurs succeed, that this process works. When you take the time to get clarity with yourself and plan your business correctly, you can avoid some of those bumps in the road that people like myself have had to face.

What It Means For You

I hope that showing you this journey of Quran Era–including the initial uncertainty of it and lack of ideation–gives you a better understanding of how many successful businesses start. You may struggle in the beginning, and you may question whether moving forward with your idea is even worth the effort, just like we did.

But when you look at the principles we've discussed here and determine that you have something that brings a meaningful solution to the world, that realization will help you stay the course.

I want you to search your heart for what you're passionate about, what drives you, and what you can do to make a difference in the world. Ask Allah SWT to put barakah in the work that you do, and that we do, because this is the form of blessed entrepreneurship I want to bring more of to this world.

Pivot

Alhamdulillah, our main assumption about the market was correct for Quran Era. But not every business will experience this. What happens when things don't work out? There are some options. One of them is called a pivot - completely changing the way in which one does something.

This was the case in my first startup. As mentioned in the previous chapter, I knew that the things I loved doing included design, startups, entrepreneurship, Islam, learning, and serving the Ummah.

It all began when a friend of mine from childhood had recently migrated to Denmark. He was looking for a corporate job, while I was leaving a corporate job. We would meet and discuss after Jumua prayers what we could do together.

My question was how to combine all the things I loved into one thing, so it would become my super *ikigai*! After studying Islam for some time, I noticed that the image of Islam and Muslims in the media was made to look negative. Sometimes, it was on purpose. Sometimes, the media would pick up only the bad news.

Understand Quran Academy

I also noticed something else. I had been volunteering at a website (www.understandquran.com by Dr. Abdulazeez Abdulraheem) for the last five years, on the side. Even though I started to redesign the original website, I have now learned new skills to turn this free educational website from a one-person part-time operation into one that hosts hundreds of teachers and thousands of Quran students in the next year, alhamdulillah.

I also learned extra skills such as marketing, team management, content production, SEO, and so many others. In fact, we increased the website traffic from 100 visits per month to over 100,000 per month by learning and implementing these skills. I noticed that there was a demand for Muslims to learn, and even pay.

Ummaland - The First Muslim Social Network

Considering this Muslim market, I came up with the idea of creating an online Muslim social network. I shared this with my friend to encourage him to join me on this journey. I would take care of the operations, strategy, design, and marketing. He would do the programming part. This is how we entered the Islamic landscape with our first startup, a social network for Muslims called Ummaland.

This startup ultimately failed. Even though we could grow our user numbers to over 400,000 members, ultimately, we could not attract investment in time to sustain our business. Later on, another friend joined us. We were three people and we were trying to do at least 50 people's work! It is normal for startups, but eventually, it caught up with us. We were also trying too many features all at one time. It had an online academy. Its own ad network. It also had a crowdfunding platform. And so many more features. It was unsustainable.

The failure was a blessing because I learned a lot from that experience. That was an important lesson I learned early on in my career: your first idea may not work, but you cannot stop there. If it doesn't work, you learn from it what you can and move on with greater determination. Looking back, we can see where we could have done better or otherwise. Hindsight is always 20/20. You can always connect the dots looking backward, not forward. Still, I don't regret any of the things we did, or even the many features we introduced. One of the features was paid ads, and people were paying for them. It was a small success within the greater failure–but learning about that one success would be a crucial catalyst for our next startup that was to come.

Halal.Ad

When Ummaland didn't work as we expected, we discussed what to do next. We now knew that Muslim business owners were willing to pay for ads. We also talked to some Muslim apps and websites with larger traffic. They were using Google AdSense to post ads on their products. The problem was that sometimes this produced non-halal ads like alcohol, banks, etc. These publishers were willing to use an alternative ad network if it was halal and paid similar payouts.

We had a purpose, a passion, and a product that served a specific market in a specific way. Ensuring all of those elements was key to success.

This is how our next startup Halal Ad Network - www.halal.ad - was born. Even though it was positioned as an ad network similar to Google AdSense, it eventually grew into a full marketing agency. After several years, Halal Ad is still in existence, and I enjoy working with other Muslim entrepreneurs and business owners in this market.

Halal.Ad is actually now not only a marketing agency but a data company as well. I am writing this book in early 2023. A year ago, Meta (Facebook & Instagram) removed targeting Muslim interests on their platform which means if you have a product or service for Muslims and you want to show ads only to Muslims, you can not any longer. For our clients and business, this presented a challenge, because the majority of our campaigns are on that platform. I reached out to all of our clients and explained what was going on. I said, "United we stand, divided we fall," a situation we could see playing out before our eyes. Then, I suggested two options:

Option 1. No one shares their audience data. Everybody loses their targeting options. We can't help any business as an agency, since targeting is crucial in advertising.

Option 2. We all share audience data with each other. We all win. We all will be able to target and grow our companies.

Alhamdulillah, all of our clients without any exception agreed to this. It was a miracle. After this unified approach, a tremendous positive impact occurred. A year ago, our company started with close to 100 million Muslim profiles. Now that more Muslim organizations and companies have joined, we have close to 400 million Muslim profiles worldwide, alhamdulillah.

With this audience, we have now also become a data company that helps Muslim companies, brands, organizations, and even marketing agencies to successfully deliver the right message to the right people at the right time.

I've come to see that that's what my *ikigai* is. That's what I love doing - helping Muslim entrepreneurs and Muslim professionals live their life with purpose, passion, and prosperity. I also love helping Muslim startups, companies, and organizations grow locally and internationally. Because I see this as my service to Allah (SWT) by serving the Ummah. It's even a form of encouraging and calling others to Islam (dawah), inshaAllah.

Deenpreneurs

As mentioned, I have talked to thousands of Muslim entrepreneurs and Muslim professionals one on one. I came to know that we have many good Muslim brothers and sisters who are genuine and want to do great things, but they need help, especially in the beginning stages of their business. They're underserved, and they need help with business guidance, digital strategy, and marketing.

Master the Four Stages

To review, the four stages of taking a product to market are:

1. Ideation
2. MVP (Minimum Viable Product)
3. PMF (Product Market Fit)
4. Growth

These four stages of taking a product to market and growing it are crucial for every entrepreneur to understand.

While most entrepreneurs build one successful business, some are masters at this. Their business becomes building businesses! And they do it again and again. Take for example Khalid Parekh, Founder, Chairman, & Group CEO of AMSYS Group. He is truly a Serial Muslim Entrepreneur. His story reveals why.

Khalid was born and raised in India in a financially struggling family. He studied Information Technology and started working as an instructor. But he knew that if he wanted to provide a better life for his family, he needed to get out of that environment. The opportunity to do so came to him as an invitation to work for his uncle as the cashier at his uncle's convenience store.

He took the opportunity and came to the United States with almost nothing. After a while, he started working at a furniture store. He not only sold the furniture, but he would deliver and assemble it as well for his customers. He worked hard.

Even though Khalid worked different jobs, he always wanted to do something on his own. One day one of his customers asked him if he could also fix his internet cable and set up a network at his house. He took up the challenge. This was during the early days of the home internet. Khalid saw this as an opportunity and started offering IT services to his customers.

He set up his first company and named it AMSYS. When I asked him about the origin of the name, I was delighted to discover that it stands for Allah, Muhammad, and Systems. He said as a Muslim, it is a reminder for him to put Allah SWT first, then the Prophet ﷺ as a priority, and then everything else. AMSYS grew from a one-man operation to a multinational IT services provider.

But Khalid didn't stop there. Today AMSYS Group has expanded its services from blockchain to energy and much more. The company is now worth $500 million. You can learn more about other AMSYS group companies here: www.amsysgroup.com

Three Things I Learned From This Muslim Serial Entrepreneur

I had the opportunity to visit and meet Khalid in person at his head office in Houston, Texas. I really wanted to know how he handles so many group companies. He shared openly how he does that. While I was there, I also learned two other life lessons. I will share them below and we all will benefit, inshaAllah.

Lesson 1. Invest In Teams. Khalid's secret to managing so many companies is that he finds someone he trusts with integrity and skills, and then gives that person the opportunity. He says most of the time, that person rises up to the challenge and outperforms and over-delivers. Khalid tells them that he trusts them and then he supports them financially, all while mentoring them on how to run the business. Then, he lets them perform, and they do.

Some of the group company directors are his old friends. Some of them are fresh graduates from universities. Khalid sees them not only as employees but as extensions of his family. They look up to him as their leader. He views the people themselves as the most valuable part of his company.

I learned a tremendous amount of wisdom from Khalid during my short stay with him. Now, I am implementing a similar strategy with the startups I work with. I scout startups with Muslim co-founders that are doing great things. I help them grow via marketing, strategy, and raising funds. It is a work in progress, but it works.

Lesson 2. Dream Big. All of Khalid's AMSYS group companies combined are worth around half a billion dollars at this point. He lives in one of the biggest mansions in Houston, TX, by a lake. He has Ferrari, Bugatti, and some other cars I don't even know.

While I was there, Khalid still came to the office early in the morning every day. He still worked as hard as everyone else. Later in the evening, we went for dinner. I asked him: "You seem to have everything. Yet you work hard as everybody else. What am I missing here?"

He replied that in the beginning, his goal was to buy his Ferrari. He reached that goal. Then a house. He did that as well. After a while, he got everything he wanted.

He said: "Once you have all the material things you want, you want something else." He was thinking about what that something else was, for him. Eventually, he found it.

We as Muslims are all aware of one of the biggest calamities of our time: refugees. We all are aware of the situation in Palestine, Syria, Uyghurs, Rohingya, and so many other places. Khalid is also keenly aware of their situations, so aware that the issue reached his heart.

Now his biggest dream is that one day he will be able to afford to buy an island just for refugees, so they can have a peaceful life. When he told me that, I was speechless for a moment. On one side, I was amazed by the audacity of the dream. On the other side, my skeptical mind was asking tons of questions: how, when, etc. I was going to ask him all these questions.

Then I remembered. He came from almost nothing, and now he is among the wealthiest people in the world. If Allah (SWT) granted all this wealth to him already, it is nothing for Him to grant him this dream as well! Who am I to question this? I made a du'a for Brother Khalid right then and there. I am also making another du'a for him as I write these lines.

O, Allah! You are The Best Giver of Gifts! You are The Wealthy! You are The Enricher! Grant Khalid his biggest dream so through him, You will enable refugees, the needy, and the orphans to have a better life. Accept this as his service to You.

O, Allah! Grant that his story inspires the rest of us: Muslim Entrepreneurs, Muslim Professionals, and Muslim Seekers from all walks of life so that we also dream big to serve You by serving Your creation. Ameen.

Lesson 3. Don't Forget Your Roots. One of Khalid's friends told me that he built a prayer place (*musallah*) in the middle of his house, where he prays Fajr and does morning deliberation (*tafakkur*) and remembrance (*dhikr*). I also saw the English translation of the Prophet's farewell sermon on his office wall. When you enter his office, you can't miss the words in bold and black: "Our word is our honor, our honor is our word." This is the line he built his business on. This is the line he stands for.

Meanwhile, as he is working towards his biggest dream, he and his companies help refugees locally, nationally, and internationally via charities and non-profit organizations. He remembers where he comes from. He remembers his beliefs and values. He remembers his roots. May Allah (SWT) keep him on this path and serve Him by serving people. May Allah (SWT) help us all remember Him all the time and where we are from and where we are going.

Du'a

O Allah! You are the Creator of all things. You are the Fashioner.
You are the Provider. Help me on my journey to find my
calling–something in line with my purpose, fueled by my passion. Make
me among the best to offer that solution to your servants, so I can
serve You in the best way possible by serving your creation.

Action Steps for Step 3 (Product)

1. Take some time to walk in nature or to reflect on how you can serve Allah SWT through your passions and strengths. Think about how you can use your unique skills and creativity to solve a problem in a way that no one else can. This may take some time, but the results are worth it.

2. If you are a Muslim Professional, based on your purpose, passion, talents, and skills, determine what kind of company or team you'd like to join. Make a list of at least 3 companies so you can approach them.

3. If you are a Muslim Entrepreneur, assemble a team along with at least one other co-founder. You can't do everything. Choose someone you trust and who can complement your skills. You need someone to bounce ideas off.

4. Next, see what form of the 12 standard forms of value your idea falls into. Then, define what numbers to track that matter in your business.

5. Decide if you are building a startup that scales to millions or a lifestyle business just to provide for your family.

6. Start with Ideation, move on to MVP, then to PMF, then onwards to the Growth stage.

7. Continue to make sincere du'a, with full hope that Allah (SWT) can work miracles for you just as he has done for others.

In the next chapter, once you are ready, we will take what you built to the market, inshaAllah.

STEP 4 ~ PROMOTION

The fourth of the seven key entrepreneurial steps is promotion. After connecting your purpose and passion with a product or service, you must create a plan to market it via promotion. Before paying for advertisements, important questions must be answered to build your marketing strategy.

There is a famous line from the 1989 movie "Field of Dreams" that says, "If you build it, they will come." For many reasons, this is no longer true in the marketing world. So many competitors are creating so much noise that whatever your product or service is, you must differentiate yourself in your promotional campaigns. Not only do you need to inform potential clients and customers about what you built, but more importantly, why you built it and what your goals are.

Many entrepreneurs tell me that they are not good at marketing. When I ask them to explain more, entrepreneurs share the same misunderstandings about marketing. They tell me that they cannot talk about their product or themselves. That is not marketing.

It is imperative to remember that marketing is not talking about yourself. Marketing is also not sales, which is another common misconception that we will discuss later. An even greater surprise may be that marketing is not even talking about your product, per se.

So, What's Marketing?

Dictionary.com defines marketing as, "the action or business of promoting and selling products or services, including market research and advertising."

Hubspot.com defines marketing as "any actions a company takes to attract an audience to the company's product or services through high-quality messaging. It aims to deliver standalone value for prospects and consumers through content, with the long-term goal of demonstrating product value, strengthening brand loyalty, and ultimately increasing sales."

I know at times some of these words could be new or difficult to understand. So here is my definition after working at least 15 years in marketing:

Marketing is, in one simple word, **storytelling**. When you are invested in your purpose, passionately staying the course, and providing a product that is a valuable and creative solution to a problem-- then you *already* have a worthy story to tell.

When you have checked all those boxes, marketing is easy. Don't worry; you will not have to devise an ingenious and amusing way to sell a product. Storytelling for marketing is simply starting from the beginning to share your entrepreneurial journey.

What makes your journey so special? True, there are plenty of products and services already available. You may be surprised to know that, within the existing noise of marketing, people want to hear why you do what you do and who you are doing it for, and they want to hear it even before hearing about your product.

We have learned marketing from the best resources and implemented it in companies to get results to make sure they work, and now you will too. Following along, you will begin to see and understand these storytelling techniques.

Golden Circle

Simon Sinek's Ted Talk "Golden Circle" is a quick and exemplary explanation of how successful companies market themselves. Sinek draws three circles and labels them from the inside out: why, how, and what.

Most people communicate from the outside "what" they do or sell, and then maybe demonstrate "how," but they rarely explain "why." This popular method is okay. It works and gives you results. But studying some of the best companies' marketing strategies reveals better methods with better results.

Sinek says that inspired people communicate their story in reverse from why (purpose) to how (passion) to what (product). He demonstrates how Apple differentiates itself from others. "People don't buy what you do; they buy why you do it," explains Sinek. Apple positions itself as an innovator who challenges the status quo. Buyers who like to feel individualistic - like rebels - feel good buying into Apple's story.

Misfits and Angels

What I have further learned is that the top brands finesse the way they talk about themselves and what they do. What do I mean by this? These brands put the buyer directly into the brand's storyline. Consider the famous Apple commercial "Think Different," which is better known as "Here's to the Crazy Ones."

Made in a very simple style, the ad features archival footage of some of the world's most famous innovators from a wide range of fields, including Albert Einstein, Martin Luther King Jr, Muhammad Ali, Amelia Earhart, Imogen Cunningham, and Richard Branson. A narration of just a 100-word count plays over the ad likening the famous personas to what they were called in their times, "....the misfits. The rebels. The troublemakers."

The narrator says, "You can quote them, disagree with them, glorify or vilify them… the only thing you can't do is ignore them. Because they change things…While some may see them as the crazy ones, we see genius."

In the entirety of the 60-second ad, Apple is never mentioned! Neither are Apple customers. The advertisement is about the type of people Apple serves: creative people, those who think differently. The ad ends with a smooth invitation to Apple's target market, "...the people who are crazy enough to think they can change the world are the ones who do." The ad suggests that if you think differently and thereby live differently, you, too, can be a champion underdog in the world.

From the Islamic perspective, I interpret this message as meaning that it is in our *fitrah* (human nature) to fight against the odds (Shaytan) and rise above this world's problems to achieve Jannah.

If we have faith in Allah (SWT) and do our best, we have the potential to be better than even the angels. Consider again when Allah (SWT) directed the angels to prostrate to humans. Our story as a species begins there. Among humans, there are those who could actually be better than angels. While the angels prostrated to humans, Iblis did not. He, to this day, thinks he is better than humans and continues to undermine us.

This, I think, creates the dynamic of the underdog (striving people) being positioned against the odds. Apple's ad taps into that by showing that the company serves exemplary people who resist the easy, common way of life.

The Prophet Muhammad (ﷺ) said, "Islam began as something strange and will return to [being] something strange just as [it was] in the beginning, so glad tidings to the strangers."
Sahih Muslim 145

Another good example of inspired storytelling is Nike. Nike's marketing does not talk about shoes. They talk about athletes, especially champions. Nike's slogan, "Just do it" speaks to the everyday champion you can be when you do not make excuses.

In your marketing case, you will discuss why you do what you do. You will speak about who you are doing it for and who you are serving. The end of your storytelling seems almost like an add-on as if to say, "By the way, this is the project I came up with." Simply tick off the boxes, and suddenly it will all come together, just by conveying *your story.*

A Muslim Example

Let's look again at the story of Quran Era. The common what-to-why storytelling is how we usually think of Quran-learning services. The Quran (what) is the most important thing to teach your children (why) because they are your responsibility as a believing parent. Usually, the how in the story is treated as an afterthought.

There are millions of companies, mosques, schools, and individuals teaching the Quran. Unfortunately, some have even poorly served their customers with repetition and aggressive practices, giving the industry a bad reputation in some cases.

Now consider instead a why-to-what marketing model for children's Quran-learning services. Why? Muslim parents want to share the most important book with their children without repeating their painful learning experiences or creating a bad impression of Islam. We believe the way we introduce the Quran to children should be the best way possible to foster a life-long appreciation for the Quran. How? The solution is a learning system that is both effective and enjoyable. What? We created Quran Era.

This story does not start with Quran Era. Rather, it first addresses why we serve and how we are serving. Only then does it suggest that if, by the way, you are in that group we serve, we have a solution for you to try?

This is exactly how our story is told in the Quran Era marketing video we created. When you begin your promotional storytelling, you can apply these same methods to your marketing channels.

Customer Journey

So how can you implement all this knowledge and use it to grow your business? In order to do that, first remember that even this is also part of service to Allah via serving His creation. One of the best ways to do that is to put yourself in the shoes of His creation—in the place of the others you aspire to serve.

When you start your business, no one really knows who you are, or why you do what you do. Your goal is to turn **Strangers** into **Visitors** (your site, blog, shop, app) into **Leads** (you get their emails, address, and any info that helps you to move to the next stage) into **Customers** (who buy your product or service) into **Promoters** (you deliver your promise so great they go and tell their friends, family, and social network). The image below summarizes this process.

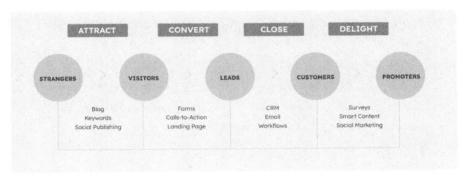

Credit: Hubspot

Introduction to Marketing Channels

While there are many ways to define marketing channels, I will share with you two categories to make it simple: **free channels** and **paid channels**.

Free Marketing Channels

Marketing channels that are free to use fall into this category. They require you to invest nothing other than time. If you hire someone to help with the marketing, you'll be investing more resources such as cash in free marketing channels.

Free marketing channels include:

- your website traffic - SEO - Search Engine Optimization
- your blog - content marketing
- your email list - email marketing
- personal circles: family, friends
- social media networks: your followers, fans, and connections.

Free channels are the first people to whom you will be telling your story. In a way, they are your test market.

One thing to keep in mind about marketing to friends and family is that even though they may see quality products and services on their networks, for various reasons, sometimes they do not buy what is being shared with them.

When doing Sales, the first people who will trust you will be Strangers. Friends will be shielding against you, and fair-weather friends will distance themselves from you. The family will look down upon you.

The day you finally succeed, paying the bill for every get-together dinner, and entertainment, you will realize that everyone else is present except the Strangers.
—Jack Ma, Founder of Ali Baba

This is why it's important to reach out widely on your social networks. While you are not ready for a large audience of strangers who have no connection to you and inclination to buy from you personally, a bit larger audience just beyond your family and friends is most effective. Marketing to people who know of you but are not too close to you is key. You can reach out broadly on your free marketing channels by posting on the social networks you already use, such as Whatsapp, LinkedIn, and Facebook.

Once you begin posting your story, then listen. Do other people react? Are they interested? Do you have orders coming from the story you have shared so far? If so, that's good. If not, you may want to ask your channels for feedback. Have conversations about your message, what is working, and what's not right. Don't belittle the feedback you receive.

Paid Marketing Channels

When your story is fine-tuned, you can expand your marketing options and begin talking to paid channels.

Currently, paid marketing channels are things like

- online ads on Facebook, Instagram, Google, YouTube, TikTok, and so on.
- TV & Radio ads
- Paid Social Media Influencers
- Joint Ventures
- Affiliate Marketing
- Billboards

In the next section, Purchase, we will go into more detail about numbers, expectations, and results. The key will be to understand your numbers. In some cases, your marketing has to make money from day one, and in other scenarios, you know that it may take months before the marketing campaign pays off. But the most important thing to know about promotion is that before you pursue paid marketing and scale it up, which you must do in most businesses, you first have to be sure that your marketing makes sense.

A Word of Caution

As the co-founder of Halal Ad Network, in the 10 years of people seeking our services, I would say that about 90-95% are not ready for marketing. Of the thousands of entrepreneurs we have talked to, we always begin by analyzing the *why* of what they are doing, which they seldom have concrete answers for.

At the same time, companies who were ready were the ones who had already launched their product and let people try it, as they often already had customers. Those who tried the product and loved it turned into repeat customers, which means the company delivered its promise. This is how you know that you are ready to go big in marketing–especially paid advertising.

When businesses are truly ready, if they have found a good way of selling, we are happy to take them on board and help them. If they are not ready, as many unfortunately are not, then we have to send them back with advice to prepare for what comes *before* the marketing stage.

This rejection is crucial because, in business, you want to ensure the value is there and comes with a promise of delivery. If we accept a client who is not ready, we cannot deliver the services to them that we have spent years developing.

I am sure that many of the clients I have turned away have found other marketing agencies who will take their money while promising the sun and moon in return. But ultimately, they will not see results because their product or service is not ready. You cannot begin marketing too soon. Everyone must invest time and effort to reach each necessary stage.

Long Term vs. Short Term

Let's return to the example of Understand Quran Academy, which I was fortunate to help grow from almost no traffic to 250,000 monthly visitors within seven years.

Why did this take seven years? We used free marketing channels in the first few years due to almost no budget. Namely, we used SEO - Search Engine Optimization.

Depending on your budget, you may use only free marketing channels or use both free and paid ones if your budget allows it. Paid channels will help you grow faster if you scale your ads sustainably. If you think you are ready for that, reach out to us at www.halal.ad and we will help, inshaAllah.

With Understand Quran Academy, I tested the product myself. I spent around a month going through their short course. It helped me to understand everything in my daily prayers by teaching me the meaning of 125 frequently occurring Arabic words as well as basic Arabic grammar.

All of this was in 20 lessons. So the promise was delivered.

However, the website didn't look good. I went through this anyway because there was no other alternative. After I went through the course and saw the results, I reached out to the founder Dr. Abdulazeez to offer my help free of charge. He was and still is a full-time professor at a university in Saudi Arabia. Understand Quran Academy was his part-time project, and there was no marketing budget. Offering to help pro bono was the least I could do, considering the wonderful service he was offering the Muslim Ummah.

Website Redesign

The first task was to redesign the website. That was the easy part since I could do it myself based on my experience, alhamdulillah. After it was done, I had to figure out how to tell people about this great course so more and more Muslims could learn to pray their daily prayers with understanding.

SEO

As mentioned, we didn't have any marketing budget. But we had some volunteers and lots of time. As this was in 2007, I didn't know much about digital marketing and so I had to learn while doing this project. I researched how to grow website traffic. One of the terms I kept seeing was Search Engine Optimization (SEO). While it may seem fancy, basically, it is optimizing your website for search engines. This involves ensuring you have readable URLs and your headings are formatted correctly, etc. You can easily find out about on-site SEO by searching Google.

What's the main benefit of SEO? In our case, it was to figure out how to get more people to the site so we could tell them our story.

To do this, one of the tools I used was Answer The Public. One of the cool things about this tool is you can find out what people are searching for on Google even by specific locations.

In our case, we wanted to find out what people searched about the term "Quran." This is what I found:

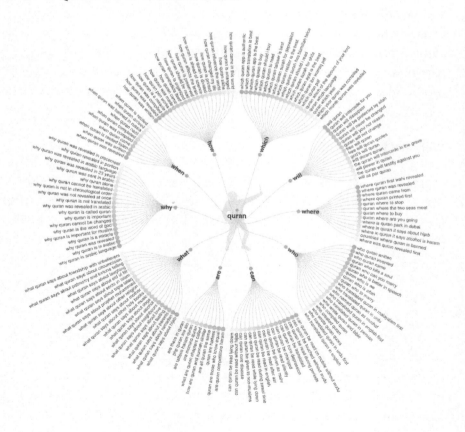

Source: Answer The Public

As you can see, these are the top questions people are searching for about this keyword, "Quran." There were hundreds of them. Then we started writing a blog article on each question. First, it was one blog article a week. Once we started seeing the traffic increase, we started writing 2-3 times per week.

Slowly, we got more visitors who turned into paying customers. Then, we could hire more team members to write articles.

Content Marketing / Email Marketing

We also started collecting emails in exchange for free access to some courses. This allowed us to start sharing our blog articles via email as well.

Here I want to note that at any time, around 1 to 3% of your target audience is in the market to buy. Most entrepreneurs spend all of their time and energy trying to convert them into buyers. In doing so, they forget or neglect the other 97%.

This is why we started collecting email addresses and we would email at least once per week to share new articles from our blog. Most of our blog articles were not promotional but educational in nature. We knew that we were fulfilling the needs of both paying and non-paying members of our audience. However, we would also send one promotional email every three email campaigns.

This method increased the traffic to the website which in turn increased the number of buyers.

Then we also began to produce social media posts with a theme. For us, each post was about a short lesson from the Quran.

Paid Ads

Once the free marketing channels were succeeding, we moved on to paid channels since we now had the funds to test. We also worked with other affiliates and created Ramadan bundles. Some of these bundles would sell hundreds and thousands in the years to come!

Fast forward to today, and now Understand Quran Academy has around 250,000 monthly visitors. The academy employs hundreds of Quran teachers and serves thousands of Quran students. The best part? They've now made their flagship Understand Quran Course, the same course I took so many years ago, free of charge. It is short and it is even animated. You can watch it on YouTube or our ad-free platform for Muslim Kids - Ali Huda.

Growth

If you think you are in the Growth stage of your product or service, it means that you:

- brainstormed and came up with the product idea
- launched your idea as an MVP (minimum viable product)
- tested your market - people who are ideal customers for your product
- your market has used it, loved it, and recommended it to others (Product Market Fit or PMF)

If you've done all of these components, you're ready for growth. When considering growth, know that there are only three ways to scale your company revenue:

1. Get new customers
2. Get customers to buy more - average order value
3. Get customers to buy more often - frequency

One of the channels we at Halal.Ad used over and over again to help companies grow at scale sustainably is paid advertising. However, before you take up this journey, you should know your numbers.

You should know how much you are willing to spend to get a new customer and how long it will take you to get a return on your ad spend.

For example, at Ali Huda—another startup we launched for Muslim kids to enjoy cartoons and shows—we tested our paid ads and managed to get a new paying client for $15 consistently. Knowing that we charged our customers $10 per month, we knew it would take only two months before we returned our ad spend. It was a good deal.

This is how we got our first 1,000 paying customers. This is the same story we presented to our Muslim angel investors (wealthy private investors focused on financing small business ventures in exchange for equity) and got our first round of funding as well to grow our startup even further.

Du'a

Before we jump on to Action Steps, let's make a du'a.

O Allah! Help me discover my story and tell it to the right people in the right way so I can serve them the best way and come closer to You.

My Lord, expand for me my breast [with assurance] And ease for me my task And untie the knot from my tongue That they may understand my speech.
Quran, 20:25-28

Action Steps for Step 4 (Promotion)

1. Know your story. Review Purpose, Passion & Product.
2. Know whom you serve. Get to know your ideal customers.
3. Determine what marketing channels are you going to use to tell your story. Free or Paid?
4. Identify which key metrics you will use to measure progress.

PURPOSE   PASSION   PRODUCT   PROMOTION   **PURCHASE**

STEP 5 ~ PURCHASE

Who is the world's best salesman, past or present? The answer might surprise you. We will get to that in a bit. However, let's learn more about the basics of Sales first.

The fifth of the seven key steps on your journey is Purchase, also known as sales. After learning how to talk about the product you are passionate about, it's time to plan your purchase. This just means how you will offer your product or service to consumers.

Sales is another sadly misunderstood stage of business, marred by the cheesy, aggressive, and tricky tactics that too many sellers have used throughout time. There is a famous saying, "Nobody likes to be sold, but they like to buy." This is absolutely true. People *have to buy* many things, but they rightfully do not like to be treated poorly by sellers.

As Deenpreneurs, we need to reorient ourselves away from negative or improper ways of selling and learn how to sell with professionalism and integrity.

Ready to Sell?

Hopefully, you have begun addressing your free marketing channels to tell them the story of what you are doing, but more importantly, why you are doing it. Your circles will begin to better know who you are and why they should join your journey.

But if you put in all this effort, learning and creating so much work, and then you do absolutely nothing with it beyond your small circles, it would be a waste. There would be no forward momentum of the value you have created. This is where the significance of purchase (also called sales) comes into play, and it is one of the core pillars of any business.

If this purchase stage doesn't happen, value doesn't exchange hands. You will not be paid. Your teammates will not be able to get paid. You will not have the funds to grow your business. And your customers also don't get to be served by your purpose and passion!

The blood supply of any business is money. To be worthy of receiving that blood, you must believe and be able to prove that you are selling the solution to a problem better than anybody else.

Suppose you have created something unique, something so phenomenal that it actually changes how things have been done. Doesn't it become like an obligation and responsibility on your shoulders to get it to as many people as possible? There is a trust (*amanah*) to pushing forward with all the blessings you have already received in your entrepreneurial experience.

Why do people buy?

The story you have identified and learned to tell in promotion is now ready to be broadcasted to people who are willing to give you their hard-earned money. Money is a storage of value. Sales happen when you prove the value of your offer; the consumer recognizes the value and agrees to exchange money for your product.

Why do people buy? Let's look at a classic example. Why does someone buy a drill? As the old saying goes, people don't need a drill, they need a hole in the wall. Actually, we can go deeper than this.

First, we need to look into these 5 Core Human Drives and why we do what we do. Josh Kaufman discusses these in his book "The Personal MBA." I have listed them below, from the basic to advanced core motives.

The 5 Core Human Drives

- The Drive to Feel (Experiences)
- The Drive to Learn (Curiosity, Personal Growth)
- The Drive to Bond (Family, Friends, Society)
- The Drive to Acquire (Material & Immaterial Things)
- The Drive to Defend (Safety & Security)

With these main drives in mind, let's return to the example of the drill. People purchase a drill so that they can drill a hole in the wall. Why? They drill a hole in the wall so that they can hang a family photo. Why? They hang a family photo on the wall so that they remember their family moments. Why? Because humans have the Drive to Bond. They have the Drive to Feel as well. It is ok if you end up with more than one drive. The more core drives you can connect with your product, the better.

Let's take a look at Quran Era. Our users are Muslim children from 5 to 12 years old. However, our clients are Muslim parents. Before we get to our users, we need to convince their parents. We have a perfect hadith for this, alhamdulillah.

The Prophet, ﷺ said, "Whoever reads the Quran, learns it, and acts in accordance with it, on the Day of Resurrection, his parents will be given a crown to wear whose light will be like the light of the sun, and his parents will be given garments which far surpass everything that is found in this world.

They will say, 'Why have we been given this to wear?'

It will be said, 'Because your child learned the Quran.'"
Al-Haakim; Al-Albaani: authentic, in Saheeh At-Targheeb

This hadith appeals to Muslim parent's Drive to Feel (being honored by Allah (SWT)), Drive to Bond (being together with their family), Drive to Acquire (that status on the day of Judgement).

We also communicate the problem of teaching Muslim children the Quran in this day and age of devices as well as games. We explain how Quran Era discovered the most fun way to teach Muslim kids how to read the Quran. It has worked for thousands of Muslim children. It will work for their kids as well, inshaAllah. This is our promise.

So, how can you utilize this new knowledge with your product? Take a moment to list out all the possible reasons that people might want to purchase your product or service. Be creative, and think outside the box.

Cost-Based Pricing

After refining storytelling, the fundamental business principle you must grasp is pricing. There are many methods to calculate the price of your product. I would say pricing is partially science, partially art.

To calculate your prices, you have to really know three things:

1. Who you are selling to
2. How much you are willing to pay for the whole process of selling your product or service
3. The best pricing method for you from among the different types of pricing (this is the most important).

One way of pricing products is based on the cost of materials and production. Few sellers use this method. They calculate the cost to make an item, then tack on a small fee for their service of providing the item to buyers. Say a pen costs $1 to make, then the producer adds 10 cents, selling each pen for $1.10. This is just one way of doing business that is neither right nor wrong. The method you choose for pricing depends on your goal.

When you add 10 cents to 100 cents, it creates a 10% margin. Such a small margin allows you to sustain your business but doesn't allow you to grow, hire a team or spend on marketing. A business with a 10% margin will remain a small business, which is fine if that is your goal. But for entrepreneurs who want to grow, I encourage them not to set prices based on costs but instead on another method of pricing that is ideal for growth.

Value-Based Pricing

You can price your product or service based on the value. Of course, this depends on your specific product and whether or not it is commoditized, meaning the specific product is available from multiple producers. For instance, say I am going to sell pens. Researching the price points of pens, I find that they range from less than a dollar to a thousand dollars. This may be shocking to hear a pen can cost so much, but it's true.

Montblanc is a 100-year-old luxury brand that sells pens that range in price from $200 to $1,000. A brand like this takes many years to grow, positioning itself as a status symbol along the way. For such high-value points, the brand's goal must be identified to become high-end and luxurious.

My hypothetical pen works well, leaving bright ink marks. It is a quality pen, but not made out of especially expensive materials or by master craftspeople, so I am okay with pricing it at $10.

I do not suggest you immediately enter a business with high price points. It takes many years to develop the value of such a price point for a commoditized item or service.

But on the other hand, if you create a product that doesn't exist yet or come up with a unique solution, then it is not commoditized, and buyers have nothing to compare your offer to. Potential buyers can only evaluate the value you are giving. For example, let's look at the Halal Ad once more.

Halal Ad has become the premiere agency in the western world that specifically targets the Muslim market. We have built up unique audience data on Muslim consumers, which cannot be found anywhere else. In this position, we know that we can increase businesses by specific data metrics by directly connecting their product with buyers who want them.

For example, if a company is making $100,000 per month, and our data indicate they can make $300,000 monthly via marketing. What is our service worth for the company? It's obvious. It is worth $300,000. So, the question becomes, how much is the client willing to pay to gain $200,000 of additional revenue? This is how Halal Ad actually puts a value on pricing. Prices are not based on the cost of materials, rather they are based on the value we give.

Now that we have discussed pricing based on cost and based on value, the next thing to review is the prices themselves.

Price Ranges

There are different types of pricing. Very low-end pricing ranges from about $1 to $9. At such prices, we can make a purchase, especially in North America, and Europe, without much thought. A few dollars is just one cup of coffee.

The next range will be around $11 to $50 maximum. This is considered mid-range. For some products and services, this medium price range may go up to $99. People need just a little bit of trust in the offering to make mid-range purchases. For some consumers, no pre-buying concern is needed here either, while other consumers may need a couple of days to consider if they value the thing enough to pay between $11 to $99 for it.

High ticket items cost over a hundred dollars, into the thousands of dollars and beyond. These big-ticket purchases are made slower, with more care. Some deals and sales take months or even years to negotiate. Each sale has a unique cycle.

Sales Cycle

Many products have a fairly simple sales cycle. First, the product is placed in a physical or online shop in a way that demonstrates why it is good. This can be done through packaging and display. Maybe there are reviews and other information presented to help customers easily make a decision on the spot.

However, other purchases are not so easy to sell. For instance, this is true if you're selling a service. In the case of Halal.Ad, we sell a customized strategy that is not like a singular item that can be added to a shopping cart and bought. There is a process by which the customer and service provider discover what services are appropriate for the client. Identifying what services we can provide, what return the client can expect, and what the applicable fees take two to four weeks. This is a longer cycle than selling a pen, but probably shorter than selling a house.

Another example that uses a different method of sales is the Quran Era app. This product does not require a lot of calls to sell and is low priced, but it still comes with its own unique sales needs.

Recall that we differentiated our product from other Quran-learning apps through our why-to-what storytelling in our marketing strategy. We address the big idea of children reading the Quran in a new enjoyable way instead of traditional painful methods. Quran Era's innovative method is based on games and activities, and most importantly, we assure parents that their children will initiate learning

Quran on their own with this app instead of being forced into unlikable learning situations.

Our pitch is already different from many other apps that use the common, less-effective method to sell their product. Others follow the model of this is what we have; it costs this much, buy it.

As you see, pricing and sales cycles vary, but no singular sales method applies to you. There are many methods, but within each, you must take the time to finesse all the points to determine what works for you best. While I cannot, unfortunately, cover all the details of every method, the intention here is to help entrepreneurs acquire the main principles of business.

Building Trust

Quran Era and all the other apps have customer reviews to help consumers make their buying choice. Our price point is low, around $9, but so are most of the other apps. So what is another way we can differentiate ourselves?

There is one tactic you have frequently seen and likely bought into, and that's the free trial offer. This is an effective method, especially for subscription-based businesses. For Quran Era, we do not trick or pressure the consumer by taking their bank card information and automatically selling them the next month of services. All we ask parents to do is to download the app, open it, and give it to their child. Children can try the games and activities for a week, and if they are excited about the experience, then parents can buy the monthly subscription.

The takeaway here is: always ask for a call to action in sales; in this case, we ask consumers just to try it out.

Raise Your Words, Not Your Voice

As Muslim entrepreneurs, we think it is a part of our service to Allah (SWT) to introduce kids to His book in the best way. Being honest, appreciating our opportunities, being generous, and taking care of what we have been given are all behaviors that are encouraged in Islam and should be directly reflected in all of our business dealings.

The youngest generation of Muslims is just as deserving of the best things as anyone else. We should not cut corners, be tricky, or even be forceful in serving them. In general, this is a huge misconception about sales, with people conflating aggressiveness and often even yelling as part of their sales pitch.

If we truly want to conduct our affairs with beauty (*ihsan*), we should raise our words, but not our voice. This means that by conducting our businesses in beautiful and honest ways, rather than forceful or off-putting ways, we will succeed.

The Best Salesman In The World

If you ask me, honestly, I believe the best salesperson in the world is Prophet Muhammad (SAW). You may disagree with me, but here are the numbers. His task was to deliver the message of Islam to his people who lived during his time and also for the generations to come, and he did so with moral beauty. There are millions upon millions of Muslims who believed in the promise of this product. More believed in his message even without seeing him in person. As we speak, the number of people who are "sold" on the idea is billions. The only other person who comes close may be yet another prophet Isa (Jesus) (AS).

But if we take into account the original message, how it was delivered, and how it is preserved over the ages, then nothing can come even close to the message he was sent with.

So why did I introduce Islam as a "product" or "promise" and the

Prophet (SAW) as a salesperson? Because we all need to learn sales sooner or later. You already "sell" every day even without knowing. How effective you are depends on your closing.

Everyone Is Selling

Sales skills are necessary for many transactions and interactions. If someone is not an entrepreneur but wants a better job, they should get better at sales. Communicating your idea effectively and efficiently to someone else, in a way that leads them to understand and relate, is sales!

These efforts are made to exchange value. If you want a better job, you must sell your value as an employee to a prospective employer.

Personally, I get very excited about sales because I really care about the efforts people make and enjoy doing my part to help them get further in their goals. That's what sales is about for me. Sales is always about solving a problem really well. You make sure the product or service works, craft and tell your story, and then ask for action from your audience.

Du'a

Before we jump on to Action Steps, let's make another du'a.

O Allah! Help me discover my story and tell it to the right people in the right way so I can serve them the best way and so I come closer to You.

> *My Lord! Uplift my heart for me, make my task easy, and remove the impediment from my tongue so people may understand my speech. Quran, 20:25-28*

Action Steps for Step 5 (Purchase)

1. What problem does your product or service solve better than anyone? At least 10 times better?
2. What is your product's promise?
3. What price range is your product or service?
4. What does your sales cycle look like?
5. Why should people trust you and your offer? (Testimonials)
6. What guarantee do you offer if your product doesn't deliver?
7. How do you sell? Online, offline, or hybrid?

STEP 6 ~ PROMISE

What does a promise have to do with the Kaaba and Zamzam? I promise I will get to that by the end of this chapter. For now, let's dive into what the Promise step is and why it is important.

In the first chapter, we did quite a bit of analysis on your purpose in life. Then we looked inwards to get to know your passion. Next, we came up with a product and service based on that purpose and passion. That product was so great–ideally, 10 times greater than what is in the market. Then we crafted our story about why we do and what we do, in order to share it with our ideal customers. We even promised that our product will solve their problem.

In this next chapter, we're going to talk more about that promise. It is the reason why people buy from you. It is what you or your product or service needs to deliver. Once you keep your promise, you not only deliver but delight (over-deliver) your customer. This is the key for your business to not only survive but thrive as well, inshaAllah.

Quran Era Promise

With our flagship app, Quran Era, the promise was the key. If a customer came to us and said "I have a child who's seven years old. He

129

needs to learn to read the Quran. Can you help me?", our promise to meet their needs has to be spot on.

In this instance, the promise from our team might look like this: We can definitely help you! Children love stories, and they love games, which is why we have combined both of those fun-filled activities with Quran learning. Using the Quran Era app, your child will enjoy fascinating stories and play fun games to make Quran learning exciting and memorable. A win-win for both parents and kids!

That's the promise! All they need is to give it a try. So the moment a customer begins the free trial, the sales process begins, and one of the core pillars after sales is called promise delivery.

Promises are great in business, but if you can't deliver on them, you will not have a successful business. It's just a simple ethical thing to do, but a lot of people just fall short here. So to deliver on your promise, you need to have three things:

1. a product that does for your customer what you said it will do
2. a product that does that thing as enjoyably as possible
3. a product that goes beyond and over-delivers

And without a great product, you can't fulfill your company's promise.

Political Promise

Many politicians today come up with fantastical promises which people believe in, and then most politicians don't deliver. That's often why people don't believe in politicians any longer.

This is a simple concept we learned as children, like the story of the boy who cried wolf. The first cry, people believed him, the second time, they still believed, but by the third time, people didn't believe him at all.

How Islam Spread In Southeast Asia

In business, being proven to be dishonest is like the kiss of death. It's hard for a company to return after losing its customers' trust.

Islam teaches us this as well. We can read stories of the Sahaba and see examples of them being honest in their work. This honesty is the same reason why people should buy from you. It is what you or your product or service needs to deliver. Islam in Indonesia is considered to have gradually spread through merchant activities by Muslim traders and the local people saw how honest they were in their dealings—in delivering their promises.

As sellers at the market, describing defects of products or discounting items and letting buyers know if there was something wrong, was a clear way to show us how important it is for us to be honest in our business dealings.

One of the things I like about the business is that I can find universal values, which mirror those that come from Islam, particularly when Allah (SWT) tells us to be honest in our dealing with people Muslim or non-Muslim.

The 80% Success Rate

Coming back to promise, in our previous example, this parent bought the Quran Era app, which gives us a short window of time for us to introduce them to our product. They need to open the app or website and start interacting. If we can get customers to actually start using our product, our success rate is then usually between 80 to 90%. So it means if someone starts a free trial with us, our success rate is approximately 80 to 90%. This means that if 10 people start the free trial, our data shows that after seven days, at least 80% will convert into paying customers.

Sticky Product

As a business owner, you have to make sense of your data. And that data will never be one hundred percent. After signing up, some people don't have time, or maybe they don't find it particularly interesting, even though we may feel that we made the most interesting product.

But if you are reaching an 80% conversion rate, know that that is very high. It's a very good mark to hit, but it's also very challenging. We call this conversion range "sticky," and the product is really sticky. In other words, the idea stuck! It worked.

In this instance, our promised delivery to our end-user was fulfilled. If we keep 80%, alhamdulillah, eight out of 10 people find this product helpful. Even though the customer is just starting our program, since they've continued past the free trial, they've converted to paid customers.

Think about it this way: **customers are pleased when they find that your promises align with their needs.** It's a simple concept, and it's easier said than done. If you don't have an exceptional sticky product, you will be unable to keep your promises. And that's why it's so important to be innovative, to have a great idea, and to understand what your purpose is before you even move into your promise, i.e., messaging.

Key To Growth

These key components are things that every entrepreneur must master. You have to tell a story, you have to make a promise and sell that promise, and most importantly, you have to deliver. If you can't do those crucial things as a business owner, it will cripple your growth and prevent customers from developing a relationship of trust with you and your business.

That trust is paramount. And if you establish it from the beginning, you can set yourself up to develop a base of repeat customers that will come back to your business again and again. This gives your business longevity and gives it what they call 'legs,' and that's one of the key ways in which you grow.

When You Overdeliver Your Promise

Even though this is an example from the Quran Era app, it's something that can apply to the lifecycle of your own businesses. If, as parents, our customers are pleased with this app and the progress that their children are having, they will tell other people. When customers are satisfied with your product or business, they become self-appointed salespeople—that's word of mouth.

And word-of-mouth is the best way to grow your business. It helps you to feel confident with your team and brings in good reviews followed by more customers. When you have an optic like this that leads to more customers and more conversions, you can also then increase your marketing. Your data has shown that customers are converting, so you can spend with more confidence, to grow your business. You can delight your investors with the successes that you're having, and everybody is happy and benefitting. And most importantly, your users are happy.

Long-Term Relationships With Clients

When it comes to the customer experience at Halal Ad, we have been very intentional in wanting to cultivate long-term relationships with our clients. This isn't done by holding them to stringent agreements, so we don't lock our clients in for 12 or 24 months contracts, as is typical with some ad agencies or networks. Instead, we have open-ended contracts. In this way, we conduct our business with excellence (*ihsan*), which rewards us with strong, fulfilling long-term client relationships.

Underpromise. Overdeliver.

We only take clients if we believe we can actually add value to their business, and you should consider doing the same. Let's look at online education, a vertical that's coming into the current business arena more and more every day. From our previous customers that are similar, we know for every dollar they spend on advertisements, we can help them earn back $3-5 in revenue. We don't promise that, because no one can promise exact sales figures, but based on our experience with past clients, we can make projections.

As a rule, we usually underpromise when giving sales projections. We may give a projection of 2X, but most of the time (about 90% of the time), we deliver between 3-5X. Clients can become anxious because we all want to see those big numbers, so by underpromising and overdelivering, those anxieties are set at ease.

But it's a process; not every client has a project ready to be scaled. Not every entrepreneur has done the work in creating their ideal customer avatar or honing in on their messaging.

So many different factors can come into play that affect your journey. And sometimes it just doesn't work, and that's ok. Countless entrepreneurs have had cherished businesses crash and burn. But you learn from it, you get back up, and you keep trying.

Care After Sale

Once you have satisfied your customer and delivered on your promise, you want to maximize that relationship. You want to build upon the trust you have established so that your customers now feel comfortable referring their friends and family to you.

This ongoing referral machine is something any company can establish and is reflected in your customer service. Remember, **customer service does not end with the sale.** After your people buy from you, how do you continue to nurture that relationship? How do you stay top of mind as the product or service in your niche so that they remember to come back and shop with you again and again? All of that falls under the umbrella of customer service.

Let part of your promise delivery include customer service agents. Their job is to help your customers succeed in receiving the promise you have outlined in your business. They are there to support your customers and address issues as they arise. You may want to offer online chat, email support, or utilize ticket support software to manage customer inquiries.

You have to realize that as a business owner, you cannot wear all of the hats. You must delegate tasks to your team so that you can continue to manage the high-level functions of the company. It may be tempting to try to be in control of everything, but without delegating, you will soon fail.

Having a team (even if it's small) of support specialists will help mitigate not only customer service issues, but it will allow you to focus on management-level tasks from the onset of your business. If you can do the things that I have outlined in this section, you can have a business that's sustainable and properly positioned to grow.

I asked a friend and fellow Muslim entrepreneur Shahbaz Mirza, an award-winning corporate and startup professional, what he can share with upcoming entrepreneurs. Here's what he shared:

1. Stick To Your Promise

During the entrepreneurial journey you will suffer from shiny object syndrome which changes direction depending on the new trends, products, and business models that are available at the time. One lesson I've learned is sticking to a core promise and the reason why your brand exists. Be bold, go against the trend, and become laser-focused on your why.

2. If It Doesn't Feel Right Don't Do It

There were many times in the journey of [my company] Ramadan Legacy and now Towards Faith when certain decisions just didn't feel right whether it be financial, business, or product decisions. If your gut is telling you something, listen to it. Looking at the facts is great but align your decisions with your identity, who you are, and your gut feeling.

3. Obsess Over Your Users

Your users are your greatest asset. At Towards Faith, we call them our companions. Their insights, support, and advice will be second to none. I remember speaking to one of our users and she provided me with advice that I would never get anywhere else. Build your product with your user, around their pain points and lifestyle, so that when you launch you achieve product market fit.

Lessons Learned from Umrah

To further illustrate the concept of promise, let's consider a story related to one of the five pillars of Islam—Hajj. If you can afford it, you should perform Hajj at least once in your lifetime. I used to have a notion that I could do it later in my life when I retired, which is a trick by Shaytan. If you can, you should do it as soon as possible. You can fulfill your Hajj while you are able.

Anyway, that notion recently changed. My friends keep telling me if you can, you should. May Allah reward them. There was still one issue. I really wanted to send my mom to Hajj before I went, out of respect. While Hajj has a long waiting list from Uzbekistan, alhamdulillah, Umrah is now very accessible. So we decided to go together to Umrah with my mom.

You may have seen the photos and even videos of Makkah and Madinah. However, they will never give you the experience of what it is like to be there. In the first five days of our visit, we stayed in the Madinah of the Prophet (SAW). We prayed every day in his masjid. We said salams to him and his companions. Like so many Muslims before me, I experienced a serenity in Madinah as I have never felt anywhere else.

Mecca is much busier, however, and Masjid al-Haram and especially the Kaaba have a kind of "magnetic" power. You personally feel and experience this power, especially when you see the Kaaba up close and do *tawaf* (circling around the Kaaba).

Men are all dressed the same, wearing two pieces of white cloth worn during Hajj or Umrah, known as the *ihram*. This symbolizes that in front of Allah (SWT), everyone is the same. He doesn't care about your external form but rather about your internal reality: your awareness of Him in your heart (*taqwa*).

I have so many memories from this Umrah with my mom. Here are two lessons about the promise of Allah (SWT) that I learned while on that journey.

Safa & Marwa

Prophet Ibrahim (AS) brought his wife Hajar and his newborn son Ismail (AS) to the middle of nowhere in the desert. As he is about to leave them, Hajar asks, "Is this your idea, or did Allah (SWT) order this?" Ibrahim (AS) replies: "Allah," to which she replies, "Then Allah will not cause us to be lost." Soon, her baby is crying. She is running to get help for her son between two hills, Safa and Marwa, in the middle of a hot desert.

I challenge you to think of any other more dire situations for a mother with her baby. Yet, she put her trust in Allah (SWT) and passed the test. Zamzam gushes forth for her and her baby.

Millions of Muslims emulate her struggle as a part of the rites they perform during their Hajj and Umrah. One thought that kept coming to my mind while running between Safa and Marwa, however unlikely it may be, is that the promise of Allah is *always* fulfilled.

The Call of Ibrahim (AS)

Allah ordered Ibrahim (AS) and Ismail (AS) to build the Kaaba. When Ibrahim (AS) completed the structure, Allah commanded him to call the people to Hajj.

Ibrahim (AS) asked, "O Allah! How shall my voice reach all of those people?" Allah told him that his duty was only to give the call and it was up to Allah to make it reach the people.

And proclaim the Hajj among mankind. They will come to thee on foot

and (mounted) on every camel, lean on account of journeys through deep and distant mountain highways.
Quran, 22:27

Even though it may not have been seen as possible to Ibrahim (AS), he simply followed the command of His Lord and called people for Hajj.

Today, millions of Muslims perform Hajj and Umrah every year. It is yet another promise delivery of Allah (SWT). So without any doubt, every promise made by Allah (SWT) will come true sooner or later.

That Promised Day is also approaching day by day. There is no doubt. The question is: Are we ready? What have we prepared?

When we reflect on the concept of promise, we soon realize that we have made a promise not only to our customers but to our Lord. That promise is that we will place Him in the center of our life. The key to our success in both worlds is keeping this promise, inshaAllah.

Du'a

O Allah, help me to keep my promise to You and the people I serve for Your sake. If I can't deliver a promise, help me avoid making that promise as well. You are the All-Knowing, All Kind.

Action Steps for Step 6 (Promise)

1. Specify what you are promising your customers when they purchase your product/service
2. List out how you will deliver that promise, from 1 to 10
3. Explore how you can over-deliver on that promise. What would a score of 15 out of 10 look like?

STEP 7 ~ PROSPERITY

Is money evil? Does money corrupt people? Can a Muslim Millionaire go to Jannah? These are all great questions. You will find answers to all of these questions before you reach the end of this chapter, inshaAllah.

We have arrived at the last section of our journey: Prosperity. Here we will talk about finance, cash, and money. We are not saving the best for last. This is the difference compared to other business courses or books available to you. Usually, if you were asked why you want to have a business, the response is to make a profit—to make money.

From a Muslim perspective, of course, money is important, but it is not the first reason why we want to build a business. We started building our business with purpose and passion and then began connecting those drives to helping and serving people. Why? Because serving people with a sincere intention is serving Allah (SWT).

Then we looked at making a promise and keeping and living your promise. If we do all of these things properly, if we take care of people in our dealings, then in turn, people will take care of us. They will support us in many ways, including with money.

You can have everything in life you want if you will just help other people get what they want. —*Zig Ziglar*

Money Misunderstandings

Before we delve into financial matters, we need to address a couple of misunderstandings about money. I want to speak specifically to the Muslim Ummah's overarching misconceptions about money. Although we are not alone in this thinking, for whatever reason, one of the things our Ummah believes is that money is evil.

'Money is bad' is something that even I used to believe for many years because I come from an impoverished family. But is it?

Let's think about money equating to bad with an accurate analogy. Take fire, for example. Is fire bad? A rational human being says, "Well, it depends." Some fires can destroy things. Forest fires, damaging explosive fires, and fires that burn people may all seem bad. But then what of fires that bake? Fires that help take food from being potentially harmful and make it edible, must be good fires, right?

This teaches us that good or bad depends on the objective of how you use a thing.

Money, like fire, water, and other resources, is not necessarily good or bad on its own. One of the best musings I have heard about money is to let money be in your hand but not let it enter your heart.

When there is money in your hand and not in your heart,
it will not harm you even if it is a lot;
and when it is in your heart,
it will harm you even if there is none in your hands.
—Imam Ibn Al-Qayyim (rahimahullah)

This wise maxim from one of our expert Islamic scholars reminds us to let the money stay in our hands. You can give money through your hand, spending for your family, yourself, or others, but do not let money enter your heart. The control has been lost when it enters your heart, and that's the problem.

We also discussed this at length with my friend Ibrahim Khan of Islamic Finance Guru on our Deenpreneurs podcast. He beautifully sums this up in his message, "Let money fill your hands, not your heart." You can learn more about it here: www.deenpreneurs.net/ibrahim

Money Is a Test

Another common belief is that money corrupts people. We hear this all the time, especially in a media-driven culture where we see people act differently, seemingly turning bad after they acquire wealth.

The truth of this matter, as I found out and you can read further about it as well, is that money does not necessarily corrupt people. Money simply amplifies what is truly already in your heart. The truth is, and you probably have seen it, that people without money can still behave poorly, and people with money can still have a good heart and avoid the trappings of luxury and materialism. And vice versa.

Money doesn't change you; it reveals who you are when you no longer have to be nice.
—Tim Ferris

Money is a big test, whether we have it or not. Allah (SWT) tells us that wealth can benefit us as we can spend it in the best manner, so He actually wants us to spend. One of the best ways to use money is to give it away. I recently experienced a telling example of this.

Barakah / Blessing

At a Reviving the Islamic Spirit (RIS) conference, I had the opportunity to talk with brother Isam Bachiri, the famous singer and songwriter from the hip-hop group Outlandish. We discussed different life matters. When we were discussing business, he kept saying "more *barakah*, more *barakah*" instead of saying "more business, more business."

What do these words reveal about his mindset—or rather, his soulset? They reveal that he doesn't look at making more money; he's looking at making more blessings (*barakah*). When we take the opportunity to sit down with people who are aware of their Creator at all times, we can learn good lessons and life skills. One thing I learned from Bachiri is to view money as if it is a tool to make more *barakah* and the source of the *barakah* is no one but Allah (SWT).

For a well-intentioned heart, money itself is a blessing of *barakah*.

Money as Gas

Another good analogy about money is from Simon Sinek of the hugely influential "Golden Circle" Ted Talk. Sinek explains that most people say they make businesses to make money, but he disagrees. Imagine your company as a car and money as gas, Sinek suggests. Why do you put gas into your car? Because you want to go to various places. The places you want to go are your vision and mission.

This analogy is brilliant because none of us would ever buy a car just to put gas into it! Similarly, you don't start a business just to make money. Your business is the vehicle to take you on your journey. As a Muslim, your journey is to Allah (SWT). It will include helping other people on their journeys as well. That's the way.

Guarding, Not Greedy

When you are at Step 7, Prosperity, it is so important to continue to be mindful of what you are doing in this business sphere. It is crucial to take care of your finances throughout all the stages we have learned.

When you are selling a product, you have to be careful of your profit margins. If your profit margin is small, it may sustain you but will not allow you to grow. If you create a thing based on value, you can have a larger profit margin. That bigger margin could be paid to you, your family, and your colleagues, to bring teams on board, and it can be spent on a lot of marketing to carry your message to the world. You should do this–if your message and your passion are good, then, of course, you should share it. Guard your finances not to be greedy but rather to be plentiful.

Cash Flow

While properly pricing yourself is crucial, even with your price efficiently set, you will very likely run into cash flow problems. I am not a financial advisor and do not want to go too far off-topic with the minute details of finance, but there are key issues you need to understand from the beginning of your entrepreneurial journey.

For instance, to sell, you must first have money to buy materials, training, or other necessities–this is where cash flow begins. Still, cash flow is always needed to continue and expand the processes of business. Even as a fully functioning business, you may be providing products or services to other companies that are going to pay you in a few months' time. If you do not have good cash flow, you cannot sell like that, and you will lose customers. In the case of our Quran Era app, if we did not take care of our finances, we could not continue on this journey to bring the Quran to so many children's hands.

Busyness With Allah

I recently heard an inspiring story from a good friend and a brother in Islam, Farooq Sayfutdin, who is originally from Uzbekistan but has been based out of Chicago for the last few years. Three years ago, he created a company after being inspired by the Ertuğrul series. He named his company Dirilis (Resurrection). There were five co-founders including him.

Brother Farooq suggested something new to his co-founders to implement into the business before they started that was definitely out of the ordinary. He said, "Look, let's make this company one that will be successful and have a lasting legacy; I want to bring in another shareholder."

His colleagues said, "What do you mean? What do you have in mind?" Farooq replied, "Let's bring Allah (SWT) as our partner, and we should give Him the majority share."

All the other team members questioned him, "What do you mean?" Br. Farooq went on, "We will let Allah (SWT) get 20% from our efforts, and we will get 18% each. We have an 80% share, and He has His share of 20%. So essentially, from our earnings, we will always take 20% and give it to a cause that would please Allah (SWT)."

It took Farooq some time to properly explain his idea and convince the other co-founders. Alhamdulillah, after his concept was understood, it was accepted by all members.

I believe that because of their generosity in implementing a charity model such as this that the business flourished and grew into such a successful venture—while they started the business with almost nothing, in only a few years it now has a multi-million dollar valuation. Alhamdulillah!

What these brothers did, led by Farooq, truly inspired me. But they didn't stop there. They also created a foundation called Alif Foundation that focuses on educating communities in the Chicago area. The funds that go toward the foundation will be used to feed the needy and educate people in the community.

Deciding to give 20% of their company proceeds to Allah (SWT)'s cause is such a touching and beautiful thing. So why am I telling you this story?

I want this story to be a lesson for myself first but for you as well. When you are doing business as a Muslim entrepreneur, you have an obligation to give Zakat. We have to give from our earnings, which in the span of a year is at least 1/40th of what we should give. There's no question about that. It is the right of the poor on us–but in the case of Zakat, scholars actually call it the right of Allah on us as well. That's how significant it is.

Is there something to learn from what Brother Farooq did, by giving more than was required? By making giving part of his business model? Of course, you don't have to give 20% to start with but perhaps start with 1%. Imagine giving 1% of your company shares and setting it aside for Allah's cause. Wouldn't that be awesome? That's something I decided to implement with our companies, and I am excited about it, alhamdulillah.

Financing the Dream

I want to encourage you to do the same or something similar in your business, inshaAllah. Finance is always a crucial part of businesses. Remember the goals you've written down and how much you want to grow your business. Depending on the level you want to grow to, you may need outside funding. If you're a small business and you want to earn between $5K-$10K per month, you may not need outside funding. But if you want to grow your business by millions of dollars and get to a billion-dollar evaluation, you will eventually need outside capital.

People ask me how to pitch investors to be able to raise that type of capital. The honest answer is: you have to take the steps I've outlined in this book; this is your only framework.

No one is just going to sit down with you and hand over a check for a million dollars for you to start your dream business. But when you can demonstrate that you've done your homework, researched your niche, and have a firm grasp on your concept, audience, positioning, etc., then people will take note. Then you will get their ear, and they will listen to what your business is about when they see you are prepared. You've prepared yourself by affirming your purpose in life, understanding what you're good at, and developing a viable product. It all comes together as one.

Stories Sell

Are you with me? You sell the story, you deliver on your promise, and you take care of your finances. If you do all these things right, you are setting yourself up for success when it comes to selling your idea to investors.

That's exactly what we did with the Quran Era App, raising multiple funding rounds. We did the same thing with another company I assisted called Musaffa–the world's first halal stock screening and trading app. I followed the same formula with that company that I've outlined for you here. These are the exact same steps I took that you can begin implementing into your business today.

All you need to do is tell your story. It's what we've done in the past which has always delivered results for us. People want to hear your story.

What I mean by sharing your story is that you should have an idea that could impact thousands or even millions of people. When you can demonstrate your impact, investors will be interested in what you have to offer. When investors get involved with startups, they know nine out of ten startups will fail. So when they do invest, they're looking for a 10X return. Investors will need to find one business that can bring them a 100X return in order to accomplish that. Even if only one of the ideas works, if it brings the kind of return they're looking for, that's good enough for them.

To deliver such returns, you need to come up with a product that actually scales. Two examples of ventures we've looked at again and again are Halal Ad and Quran Era. Halal Ad is a service company, so we cannot scale there. But Quran Era could be scaled exponentially because we created a digital product with no cap on potential revenue.

Building With Millions In Mind

Whether Quran Era has 10,000 customers or 100,000 or 1,000,000, we can accommodate them without changing our business model because our software is scalable and can serve people anywhere in the world. This is why we raised funds for Quran Era, which we intend to continue inshaAllah because we want to reach millions of kids around the world.

But the journey is neither simple nor easy. If you're a founder, be prepared that this journey will be a long one. This is why I stressed the point of you doing something you care about, something that you love. That love will allow you to bear the difficulties you are bound to encounter in your business. **You will be able to work hard to overcome the hurdles because you are striving for something that you love.**

Team Building

To make your business more success-focused, you will need team members to complement your journey. And to do that, you may have to shift your mindset.

You don't want to be the person that says, "That's my company, I want to own everything!" You want to be open-minded and receptive to welcome opportunities coming your way. And yes, those opportunities may come in the form of co-founders, partners, investors, team members, etc. And those people who may enter your company may initially cause your piece of the pie to be just a little bit smaller than what you started out with.

Pie vs. Brownies

When advising startups and their co-founders regarding shares and equity, usually the pie analogy is used. For example, new team members share a piece of the pie.

By nature, usually, humans are not good at sharing, especially if there is only one of something to go around. Even though that pie gets bigger over time, our lower selves often tell us that there is not enough.

What I discovered is that brownies, rather than pie, are a better way of explaining shares. Let me explain. Instead of pie, I usually say, "Your company is here. It is a piece of brownie. You invite others and all work together. One brownie multiplies into 10 brownies, for example."

Will you be willing to share a piece or two with others? Most of the time, the answer is yes.

What if the founder still doesn't want to share? Then you don't really want to work with that person anyway. Behind any great company is a great company (of people).

Expanding Our Minds

Human beings are unfortunately often short-sighted with short-term thinking. For business dealings, we must train ourselves to shift from short-term to long-term thinking. Consider how we generally think about money—recall Sinek's car and gas analogy. Your business is a car, and money is gas. When people buy their car, they are not thinking, '*I am buying this car to buy a lot of gas.*' They are thinking about going places. But they do have to buy a lot of gas to do that.

Conversely, people do obsess about money, and that is a problem. Recall that money is a storage of value; money enables things to happen. It's not meant to be an obsession.

What you **should** obsess about is your journey and your purpose. Isn't it best to obsess about how you will serve Allah (SWT) by serving His creation?

Money Can Buy Happiness, But Up to What Point?

According to research by the New Economics Foundation, each person has a monthly income bracket where they live comfortably. Their research focused mainly on Western countries. The bracket ranges from $75,000 to $120,000 per year. Let's even take the upper end and say if you make $10,000 per month, you can live comfortably. If you make lower than this, it would cause you distress since there will be a shortage of money to provide for your family. On the other hand, if you try to make more than this, it will take away from other things in your life. For example, spending time with your family.

Once you reach a certain limit of income, your goal should no longer be income. Rather, your focus should be to move your cause forward–i.e., why you do what you do and how many more people you could help. Also, remember to give away a portion of your earnings as Zakat and charity.

Redefining Meaning

Many of us live life on autopilot. We can barely think about our journey and higher purpose when we are stuck in a holding pattern, as many people are. Many people go to their nine-to-five jobs, and even though they may go to the mosque once a week, they do not feel fulfilled.

Some even tell me, unfortunately, that they dream of being involved in low-paying or no-paying nonprofit work. I say 'unfortunately' because they do not see the greater picture. Their short-sightedness only allows them to consider that the alternative to their bleak situation is a dreamy image of doing nonprofit work.

Before even jumping to that end of the spectrum, did they actually ask themself: "What am I good at? How can I add value to my efforts?" Perhaps they are actually doing good jobs that provide value to their communities.

This type of thinking is similar to the all-or-nothing thinking of entrepreneurs about not wanting to take on co-founders or partners. People do not acknowledge their passions and instead, let their minds leap from their current positions to a fantasy about being a peace worker or ocean saver. They have not even considered what skills are involved in nonprofit work to then recognize that theirs do not match up; they may not even be suited for that field.

The point here is challenging ourselves to expand our mindsets to really think about how we can best serve with our skills—serve Allah (SWT), others, our family, and ourselves. Imagining that that service is not related to developing our unique talents and skills is a missed opportunity to become the best giver, and servant, that we can be.

Among the Best Rich Muslims

Another faulty thinking I see among Muslims involves ideas about the Sahaba and money. Some of the best companions of the Prophet Muhammad (SAW), such as Abu Bakr and Uthman (RA), were rich people. Somehow, many people don't seem to know that.

There is also this idea that the Prophet (SAW) was a trader as an employee of Khadija (RA) and later, he chose not to deal in such things. Actually, a lot of the Sahaba were tradespeople, and they were very rich, influential people. We know that they still went to Jannah. How can Muslims think badly of money, when we should know that some of the Sahaba were wealthy business people and were still good Muslims? In fact, some of them were among the best Muslims ever! As long as you have the right intention and operate in a halal manner, then as Allah (SWT) said, this is your form of service. Let me share another story.

Uthman Ibn Affan (RA) owns a hotel in Madinah today

The companion of the Prophet (SAW) and the third Khalifah owns a hotel in Madinah? He lived 1400 years ago. How come he owns a hotel nowadays in Madinah? Let me share the full story with you.

The early Muslims (Muhajirun) settling in Madinah after the migration struggled to find basic needs such as water. The most drinkable water came from a well in the city named Rumah, but the Jewish owner insisted on charging the Muslims, even for a handful of water.

In order to help the Sahaba - companions, the Prophet (SAW) asked the owner to sell him the well in exchange for a garden in Jannah. He refused the offer and only asked for money.

When Uthman ibn Affan (RA) heard that Prophet (SAW) offered the reward of Jannah for whoever could secure the well for the community, he went to the owner and placed an offer to buy it. The owner declined once more because he wanted to keep making money. Uthman asked him to sell at least half of it or rent the well to him for alternate days.

The owner agreed thinking of an immediate pay-out as well as ongoing income. Unsurprisingly, on his day, Uthman would give away the water for free to anyone who came. This resulted in everyone going to draw water from the well on Uthman's day, leaving the owner with no customers. Realizing his lack of options and to salvage what financial benefit he could, the owner offered to sell his share of the well to Uthman, who readily agreed to a price of about 20 thousand dirhams. Uthman then assigned the well as a Waqf - endowment in Allah's name. A Waqf for all Muslims to drink freely.

Later on, one of the companions came to Uthman and offered to buy the well for double its price. However, Uthman continually asked him to raise his offers, without accepting any. When the Companion finally asked him who would offer a higher price, Uthman responded "Allah."

The following decades saw date palms start to grow around the well.

Subsequent rulers over the centuries attended to and cultivated more of them. Nowadays, the dates from these palms are sold in markets and the proceeds are divided into two: one half is distributed amongst orphans and the poor, and the other half goes into a special bank account in Uthman ibn Affan's name, overseen by the Ministry of Endowments in Saudi Arabia.

Uthman ibn Affan's hotel construction site

The funds in this account have been used to buy land in the central area of the city next to the Prophet's mosque along with the construction of a hotel. The land is also officially registered in the local municipality under the name of Uthman ibn Affan (RA).

The hotel is now ready and accepting guests. It is estimated to generate around 50.000.000 Saudi riyals (around $13.000.000) per year.

Half of the revenue is distributed among the poor and orphans by the Endowment Minister of Saudi Arabia while the other half is deposited in Uthman ibn Affan's (RA) bank account for future charitable purposes.

This story gives me goosebumps every time I read it. What a blessing for Sayyidina Uthman (RA). The Prophet (SAW) promised Jannah for this well. Uthman (RA) already earnt it by buying this well and making it available for Muslims. That well keeps generating more barakah for him even long after he is gone. The wealth from the well keeps growing to the point Uthman (RA) owns now a hotel, many plantations, and date palms that keep giving even more. Even today you can walk into a bank in Saudi Arabia and can add funds to his account so your money also will be used in his waqf - endowment.

This is one of the most beautiful stories and this is what happens when money works for you, not you work for the money. It all started with a sincere intention to earn Jannah.

Du'a

O, Allah! You are The Wealthy (*Al Ghaniyy*) and You are The Enricher (*Al Mughni*). Provide for me wealth full of Your blessing that fills and flows from my hand to my family, the orphans, and the needy. Never allow it to reach my heart, so You are always pleased with how I spend this wealth You provided.

Action Steps for Step 7 (Prosperity)

1. Do you view money as good or bad? Why or why not?

2. Find out the amount of money you need to live a good life per month and measure how close you are to your target.

3. Decide on an amount you are willing to give every month, week, or day, even if it is as small as $1 or less.

PEACE

What do we all want in life? What is success? What is true happiness? What is joy? What is peace?

This is the last chapter of the book. We went through the journey together to come to this point. Typically, you will be in one of these three situations by now.

1. **You made it! Mabrook!**
    You discovered your Purpose and Passion then turned it into a Product (or joined a team) that solves a problem for people. Then you Promoted it. They Purchased it. Your product delivered its Promise. You live in Prosperity. You make a great living doing what you love. You provide for your family. You share your wealth with your community and those who are needy and the orphans as well. If this is the case, may Allah bless your journey and your story even more. Please, reach out to me via email: salam@halal.ad. Maybe, we will invite you to our podcast to share your story, iA.

2. **You are on your way.**
    You have started on your journey. You have come through

some steps. You are not quite there yet. It is ok. May Allah (SWT) keep you consistent on your journey. If you need help beyond this book, visit www.deenpreneurs.net/journey to learn more. I also offer group coaching or 1 on 1 help.

3. **You have not started yet.**
   Maybe you read the book just to entertain yourself. It is ok if this is what you want. Maybe you don't believe it will work. Maybe you don't believe that it will work for you. Maybe you are afraid that you will try and you will fail again. I completely understand. I have been there many times. Maybe you worry too much as I did. What do other people think? What if I start but do not finish again?

If you're in the third category, don't give up hope yet. Keep reading.

I want to share with you that one thing I realized that really changed how I started looking at everything is that we modern human beings think too much about ourselves. I do this. I do that. I… I… I…

Fear of Flight

Let me share one last personal story with you, about a fear I developed of flying on airplanes. In the beginning, I didn't mind flying. After a while, maybe once I became a father or maybe once I started establishing myself and gained wealth, I started to become anxious whenever I flew on airplanes. I would sit on the plane hoping that the flight would end as soon as possible. Seconds turned into minutes. Minutes turned into hours. Hours felt like days. It felt like any minute, the plane would fall down. My life would be over.

I would try to watch movies to kill time. I would try to think of anything else except the fact that I was flying a plane. I would do anything. But the reality would always kick in. The loud sound of the plane engine would remind me of where I was, over and over.

But we can only worry to a certain extent. At some point, I had to make a decision. I could either keep avoiding the biggest elephant in the room and keep doing this to myself or talk to the elephant. Flying a plane could become a bigger nightmare, or I could face my fear once and for all.

So I started asking questions: Why am I so afraid of flying? What bothers me so much?

The answer came back fast. I was afraid of a plane crash. I would die. I would lose all that I did so far—there it was. I was afraid of losing whatever I gained.

I reasoned with myself. I said, "Actually, flying is safer than driving a car." Another part of me would reply, "Well, if you are driving, then you are at least on the ground even if something happens. Now you are in the air. If something happens, this is it."

Then I realized the root cause. In the air, I had no control. However, I felt secure and in control on the ground. But was that really true? Of course not! It was a False Evidence Appearing Real-FEAR. The root cause was that I thought I was in control on the ground, but not in the sky.

In reality, it is Allah (SWT) who is always in control. Not I, me, or myself. Ever. Whatever He wills is going to pass, whether I worry or not. It is out of my control. It has always been out of my control. The real question was: Am I ready if I die today?

Once I realized that Allah (SWT) has full control, I began to experience relief. Everything is in His hands. Whatever He wills will happen. All I can control, with His help, is how I react, and how I feel. Slowly but surely, I started flying without much fear again. I will get anxious now and then again. But I remember that He is in control. And I remember the bigger, more important question: Am I ready if I return to Him today?

I share this personal example because it reminds me of how many people live their lives. They avoid reality out of fear. They escape to different realities through drugs, alcohol, games, smoking, or any other escape. They accept defeat and die spiritually, emotionally, and intellectually before they die physically.

What if there is a better way?

The Infinite Game of Life

"The Infinite Game," is a 2019 book by Simon Sinek that applies ideas from James P. Carse's similarly titled book, "Finite, and Infinite Games."

The book is based on Carse's distinction between two types of games: finite games and infinite games.

As Sinek explains, finite games (such as chess and football) are played with the goal of getting to the end of the game and winning, while following static rules. Every game has a beginning, middle, and end, and the final winner is distinctly recognizable.

In contrast, infinite games (such as business or life) are played for the purpose of continuing to play rather than to win. Sinek claims that leaders who embrace an infinite mindset, aligned with infinite play, will build a stronger, more innovative, inspiring, and resilient organization.

Now that we have the terms defined, let me share how I have redefined the concept of the Infinite Game for myself. I don't personally agree with playing for the purpose of just continuing to play. Instead, I still take it as a game but with the aim to win not only in the short run but in the long run as well. This is what our Prophet ﷺ also taught us in this du'a which we recite every day after our daily prayers:

Our Lord! Grant us the best in this life and the next life. Save us from the Fire.

Quran, 2:201

So how can you play the Infinite Game of Life as a Muslim?

The 7 Paradoxes

The following seven rules may not make sense if you look at life as something like a Finite Game. However, in the long term, it all makes sense in the Infinite Game of Life.

1. Surrender for freedom
Willingly surrender to Allah (SWT) to be free. This is not the freedom of your body, heart, or even mind, but the freedom of your soul. Usually, surrender means giving up. But not in this case. You are giving up your worldly desires in the short term to win in the long term.

2. "If you are grateful, I will certainly give you more…"
Allah (SWT) makes this promise in the Quran (14:7). It is all about an attitude of gratitude. Whenever you want more in your life, find contentment in what you already have and thank Allah genuinely. Watch what happens next.

3. Give more than you take, to experience more joy
If you need something, of course, you should satisfy that need first. Once you are done, you don't need to keep taking even more. If you give now to satisfy someone else's needs, you will feel more joy than if you keep taking for yourself.

4. Give and Allah (SWT) will give you back even more
If you keep reading the Quran, you will keep seeing this one message over and over again: give to the needy and give to the orphan. In the short term, you may think, why give? I will keep it to myself. I worked for it. If you really think about it, it all belongs to Allah. He just provided for you. Once you satisfy your need, not your desires, then give. Do you know what happens when you give? You will not only feel good beyond anything in this world, but Allah will give you back even

more. You may not believe it or it may not make sense. But give it a try. Up your game. If you want to hack your giving to another level, as Sh. Haitham from UK says give on someone else's name. You both get the same reward.

5. Win by helping others win

In a Finite Game, there is only one winner. For you to win, your opponent must lose. In the Infinite Game of Life, you win by helping others win. The Prophet ﷺ said that anyone who guides others to do a good deed will receive a reward equal to that of the person who practiced it [*Sahih Muslim*].

6. Motion to emotion

Some people think that they are not feeling well enough today to take action. They think emotion comes first, and then motion. In reality, the opposite is true. First, you take an action or motion, then you will get an emotion. Give it a try.

7. Journey & Destination

Some people enjoy the moment without worrying about the future, while others are waiting for a better future while forgetting about the present. Which way to go? What if there is a middle path? What if I told you that the world is "perfect"? Before you begin to count how many problems there are, let me explain. Imagine you want to create a simulation program to test which human beings are better at taking action, rather than just making empty promises. I challenge you to come up with a better alternative than where you are at the moment—this very life, this very reality that you are experiencing here and now. SubhanAllah.

So this world is "perfect" for what purpose Allah (SWT) created it for. Everything is from Allah (SWT) to test us. Once you realize this, you don't need to take everything personally. Your goal is to become a *Nafs Al-Mutmainnah*—a soul at peace, here and now, with whatever condition you are in. So you enjoy both the journey and destination as well, inshaAllah.

Long-Term vs. Short-Term

As humans, we all want good. Unfortunately, most of the time it is for the short term. We are always looking for a shortcut. Most of our problems would go away if we focused not only on the short term but also on the long term as well. Let me give you an example. When you are hungry, you eat fast food. It fills your stomach for the short term. However, it is not good for you in the long run. It would be better to eat healthy food which is good for the short and the long term. However, to do so nowadays requires planning, mindset, and hacking your habits which is not easy.

The same applies to what we do for a living, what we read, what we watch, etc. In a nutshell, we are looking for shortcuts throughout our life. I am not saying that we shouldn't. However, we should make sure that we take into account the long term as well. Long-term thinking will bring out long-term results even if it starts with a sincere du'a and small action.

Tiny Act. Huge Impact.

The concept of a tiny act bringing about a huge impact reminds me of the story of Imam Mustafa Khattab. He shared his story with me for our Deenpreneur podcast where you can listen to the full story. Here is the short version.

While growing up in his village, none of his siblings or Dr. Mustafa went to school. There was no school in his village. His family thought that kids are better off just helping with farming and taking care of the cattle.

His mom insisted that at least one of her children should go to school even though that child would need to travel to the next village every day to attend school. That child was Imam Mustafa Khattab.

MashaAllah, he studied so well that he eventually went on to study at Al Azhar University. After graduating, he relocated to the United States and started working as an imam at a masjid. After a while, he relocated to Canada where I got to know him in person and we became good friends, alhamdulillah.

If the story ended here, it would still have been pretty good. Imagine coming from a village where there are no schools to becoming an imam and relocating to North America.

Actually, the story gets even better. During his time in the West, he got to know the English translations of the Quran. Unfortunately, some of them were translated into the old Shakespearean language. Other translations were using more difficult words in the translation. He wished there was a simple and clear translation of the Quran into English. When he couldn't find any, he took up the challenge himself. The end result was The Clear Quran. This translation has sold millions of copies in North America and is now even the default translation on **www.Quran.com**, alhamdulillah. Imam Mustafa is now writing a series of books, including "The Clear Quran Tafsir for Kids" which is one of my favorite books to read with my own children.

Imam Mustafa's work has already impacted millions. It will also impact millions more, inshaAllah. This huge impact on the Ummah all started with his mom's tiny act. May Allah (SWT) accept this from them both and help the rest of us get inspired and take action.

Peace by Piece

We all want success. We all want happiness. We all want joy. Eventually, we all want peace. But how to get there?

Life is not happening to you. Life is happening for you.
—*Tony Robbins,*

In the beginning, you live as if life is happening to you, almost in victim mode. You may see the world at fault. You may blame everyone but yourself. Then you get responsibility and you start taking action. You begin to live as if life is happening by you.

But there is another possible level. If you then surrender to The Ever-Living, you will feel like life is happening through you. The world is "perfect" for the purpose He created it for. You are just living in contentment, dwelling in the presence and grace of the Divine. You know everything is from Allah and to Him all will return.

Shukr. Sabr. Dhikr. Taffakkur.

If something good comes your way, you are in *Shukr* (thankfulness) mode. You say alhamdulillah.

If something bad comes your way, you are in *Sabr* (patience) mode. You say alhamdulillah.

When not in *Dhikr* (remembrance), you are in *Tafakkur* (contemplation) mode. You contemplate the signs of Allah.

In between, and along the way, you are in Dhikr mode. You remember Him. You say alhamdulillah, subhanAllah, Allahu akbar. You remember Him.

Do you remember the story of when Allah (SWT) said to His angels that He will create a representative on Earth? Let's consider it, in closing, one last time.

The angels asked why He would create a creature that would spread corruption and shed blood, to which Allah (SWT) replied that He knows what they do not know.

He created Adam (AS) and asked the angels to bow down to honor Adam's status above them. The Giver of Gifts (Al Wahhab) gifted our Father Adam (AS) with knowledge, soul (breathed out of His Spirit), free will, and so many other countless gifts.

Even though we human beings are not perfect, even though we make many mistakes, and even though we fail many times, those who sincerely want to walk towards Him will be shown the straight path. They will be given a rope of hope. Those who cling to it and hold on to it for their dear life will eventually reach Him, get to know Him, and see a glimpse of what is yet to come while on their journey even before they reach their final destination, inshaAllah.

Each of us also receives these gifts from Him through our Father Adam (AS). Each of us got the same invitation to claim and be among the best human beings and the best of creation. Are we ready to accept it?

So what is true happiness? What is joy? What is peace? As you consider these questions for yourself, I will leave you with this beautiful speech by an extremely beautiful person, Shaykh Muhammad Saeed Ramadan Al Bouti—a speech he made for the Most Beautiful. He said:

"What is happiness? It is when you love The One Who loves you. And you will only love Allah because He loves you. So if you feel attracted to love Allah, know that Allah is The One Who loves you.

When love embraces love, the love of Your Creator for you embraces your love for Him; that is true happiness. Higher than anything, even entering Jannah..."

Everything we do is to reach Allah's love for us.

I know you're tired but come anyway, this is the way. It's your road, and yours alone, others may walk it with you, but no one can walk it for you.

Everyone has been made for some particular work, and the desire for that work has been put in every heart.

Stop acting so small. You are the universe in ecstatic motion.
—Rumi

Let's make one more du'a before we continue on our journey.

O, Allah! You are The Opener (*Al Fattah*). Open our hearts, and open our minds to Your signs to seek You and find You. You are The Holy & Pure. Purify our souls. You are The Expander. Expand our souls and grant us knowledge that will benefit us here and in the Hereafter. Guide us to the straight path to You so we find ourselves, our purpose, and our passion to serve You by serving Your creation in the best way. We ask from Your generosity that You grant us success so that You will write us down among the best of Your creation. Ameen.

This is not goodbye. It is an invitation.

There is a knock on your door…

Guess Who is knocking…

JOURNEY

Alhamdulillah. I am grateful for every step of my journey. It started with a boy fighting for his survival in the middle of nowhere. Fast forward to today, Allah (SWT) not only granted me more than what I asked Him, but He also gave me the opportunity to help others as well.

Ten years ago, I made a dua not knowing what to do next. But one thing was clear. I had to submit and surrender fully to Him. There was no other way. Since then I have been on this journey. I am among the first to admit this is not easy. At times, you feel like giving up. But if you ask me, I sincerely believe that this is the journey.

Because the only journey worthwhile is finding yourself.

Once you find yourself, you will find The One. Once you find The One, you have arrived.

Until you get there... Destination is important. Journey is important. So is the company. You don't have to go through this alone. Start here to join like-minded and like-hearted Muslims on a similar journey: www.deenpreneurs.net/journey

I'll see you on the path. Until then... Salams. Peace.

Printed in Great Britain
by Amazon

30484670R00096